I Have Risen   ESSAYS BY AFRICAN-AMERICAN YOUTH

I Have Risen

ESSAYS BY AFRICAN-AMERICAN YOUTH

CAP CHARITABLE FOUNDATION   CHARLOTTESVILLE, VIRGINIA

This project was made possible through
the generosity of the CAP Charitable Foundation.
All proceeds from the sale of this book will go
to the Ron Brown Scholar Program.

Contents

8 **Preface** *Sybil Fix*

11 **Foreword** *The Honorable John C. Thomas*

13 **History** *Michael A. Mallory*

Essays by African-American Youth —

117 **Ron Brown Scholars** *1997–2005*

126 **Acknowledgments**

127 **Ron Brown Scholar Program**

127 **Council on African American Affairs**

128 **Photography Credits**

16 Caprice Gray

18 Kelly L. Lee

20 Julian Miller

22 Brandon L. Nicholson

24 Nakiya K. Jones

26 Delbert A. Green II

28 Wendy F. Francois

30 Morgan K. Dooley

32 Lindsay Lally Cothrine

34 Kareemah Love Sabur

36 Immanuel R. Foster

38 Katori Hall

40 Brent E. Cash

42 Preston Scott Copeland

44 Miya Nicole Cain

46 Ihotu J. Ali

48 Jessica Larché

50 Dorothy Loretta Ann Smith

52 Caleb Franklin

54 Antonia J. Henry

56 Lordserious J. Watson

58 Derick Gross

60 Ellen Tachiewaa Yiadom

62 Miles Alexander Johnson

64 Marquise J. McGraw

66 Crystal Paul

68 Alexandra Carmel Wood

70 Robert J. Smith III

72 Autumn Joy Anderson

74 J. Paulson Tuffet

76 Samuel Zenebe Alemayehu

78 Victor A. Davis

80 Veronica H. Threadgill

82 Brandon L. Cook

84 Misha M. Mutizwa

86 Jamar Campbell

88 Morgan G. Harper

90 Ilisten M. Jones

92 Errol C. Saunders II

94 Angela A. Smedley

96 Maria I. Velazquez

98 Damian Williams

100 Anahad O'Connor

102 Nneka Madu

104 Gerald "Jay" Williams

106 Jamaal Anthony Young

108 Sparlha Swa

110 Carmelle T. Norice

112 Myia A. Alston

114 Eric S. Teasley

Dedication

I Have Risen is dedicated to all Ron Brown
Scholars, past, present and future, to the staff
of the Ron Brown Scholar Program and the
Council on African American Affairs, to Ron
Brown Scholar Program Selection Committee
members and volunteer readers, to all those
who have come in contact with the program
and helped make it what it is today, and to
all people who have struggled and have risen.

Preface

Sybil Fix

Editor

WHEN I WAS INTRODUCED TO THE IDEA OF assisting in the publication of a book of essays written by a group of African-American high school students, I was excited and intrigued. I saw the project as an expression of my commitment to better understand the critical issues of race and education in our country and of my desire to contribute to the discourse about them. On a very personal note, I was also deeply honored, in part because the person who introduced me to the project, Dr. Robynne K. Chutkan, is among the most important people in my life. Robynne is black, and I am white, and since college, where our friendship began, I have had the privilege of her prism to guide and enlighten much of what I know and feel about race in America. I was honored, therefore, that she would recommend me to handle such important work.

I didn't expect, however, for this project to turn into one of the most moving and inspiring experiences of my life, and I am profoundly grateful for it.

I Have Risen is the commemoration of the tenth anniversary of the founding of the Ron Brown Scholar Program, an endowed college scholarship fund that rewards African-American youth for excellence in academia, commitment to community service, and leadership potential. These are the Scholars' essays.

Many of the writers of these essays are kids whose lives have been scarred by poverty, homelessness, danger, family ruin, and despair. Nearly all of them, it seems, know the pain of bigotry and racism and the struggle to find the right place for their shade of color. But these young adults don't match the stereotype of the statistics to which our society, sadly, has grown so accustomed. Indeed, they defy those statistics with their every pore and breath. And that is what makes their words so relevant and important.

These essays were written when the Scholars were 16 or 17 years old, applying for college admissions and scholarships, among them the Ron Brown scholarship. Some tell stories of experiences – some harrowing, some funny – that shaped their lives and beliefs. Others tell of dreams and aspirations of doing something that will change a piece of the world. Others voice outspoken cries against injustice, racism, or inequality. Regardless of where or why they were written, across the board these essays unveil the making of a certain kind of human being – thoughtful and sensitive to the world, with a deep-seated concern for others and a visceral sense of purpose and responsibility. At a surprisingly early age, these youth look out onto the world as a common stage and recognize the importance of the role they are called to play.

Now studying at the best schools in the country, these courageous black youth are readying themselves for lives of service and contribution, of meaningful endeavors and pursuits to better the lives not only of their families and children, but of families and children worldwide.

Although many of them sprout from tremendously difficult challenges and experiences, their writings are not tales of woe. Be it the incarceration of a family member, violence or hunger in the home, the death of a friend or the abandonment by a parent, these kids have transcended their personal tragedy and, in fact, found within it the power of their inner possibilities, timeless and selfless. Devoid of victimization – indeed, fully aware of the courage of personal responsibility – in their predicament they find their connection to the rest of the world and the inspiration to make it better.

Ever cognizant of their place in history, and ever mindful of their ancestors' and people's role in time, they forge bridges between past and present like bold links in a chain, carrying forth a sense of reverence for the past yet an unbridled enthusiasm for the future. They are children of today, forged in the darkness of the shadows of yesterday, but somehow, almost miraculously, already drinking in the sunshine of tomorrow.

It is that tomorrow in the making that we celebrate in these essays, appropriately accompanied by beautiful black-and-white portraits of the Scholars taken by a group of award-winning photographers whose work we were lucky to secure for this project. Included in the book is complete information about where the essay writers are now and what they are doing, and a complete list of all Ron Brown Scholars to date. Selecting the essays to be included in the book among all the application essays written by the 181 Ron Brown Scholars over the years was a difficult process; in no way is the result intended to diminish the accomplishments of the other equally deserving Ron Brown Scholars. These were simply the most compelling essays.

We hope these small windows into the lives and souls of these young adults, some humorous, some tragic, all somehow moving, will be sources of reflection, introspection, inspiration, and gratitude. Certainly, if these youth used no excuses, for the rest of us there are no excuses for not being the best we can be as people, contributors, and fellow citizens.

I hope this book will inspire African-American youth nationwide, in desolate rural corners and inner city crevices haunted by despair and hopelessness, to dream of a better future and fight for it. Beyond that, I hope this book will inspire all readers to participate in a world that cries

out for commitment, empathy, and leadership.
Indeed, this group of young adults exhorts
us to tend, finally and forcefully, to the social
plague of racism, to the lack of commitment to
educate poor, African-American youth, and
the lack of commitment to education in the
African-American community. Perhaps as only
young eyes can, they point us to an inarguable
truth: That all of us must participate to help
make the thankless charge of growing up black
in America less difficult and hurtful. And if
we want African-American youth to excel and
contribute because of rather than in spite of the
world that surrounds them, we of all colors
ought to heed their profound words.

The essays, which were minimally edited, don't
need to be read in any particular order, and,
in fact, they follow no particular order. Each
stands alone as a jewel plucked from a crown of
different hues, each with its own voice and
sense of self. You can pick a page a day, if you
wish, or a page a night; regardless, you can
be sure to be changed – inspired, enlightened,
touched, and, perhaps, improved – by these
young voices. Without a doubt, they will grow
to influence not only the policy of this country,
but its intellectual and social life for decades
to come.

We will all be better for it, and we thank them.

Foreword

The Honorable John C. Thomas

Ron Brown Scholar Program
Selection Committee

Some of the young people featured in this book have overcome obstacles that would cause most people, young or old, to give up, to give in, to quit: Bullet-ridden neighborhoods, gang-infested schools, close contact with drug users and alcoholics, living on the run, moving from foster home to foster home. Yet they excelled.

Others come from more stable backgrounds – two-parent homes, safe communities, supportive social structures – and they have excelled.

But all of these young people have confronted the many distractions of these times: Peer pressure to be "cool" instead of being scholarly, ridicule from others for trying to get ahead in school, a sense of isolation as they persevered while others fell behind.

On top of all that, they have confronted the very special challenges that face African-American youth: Being one of only a few blacks in the class; being accused of trying to be white because of trying to learn; being looked at by white class-mates for *the* black view of things.

Despite the things in life that have pushed or pulled their peers away from academic excellence and community service, the young people featured here have committed themselves to the highest levels of intellectual attainment and the broadest reaches of public service.

The Ron Brown Scholar Program has brought these remarkable young people in touch with each other in the hope that together they will strengthen and encourage each other and work together for the rest of their lives to change the world. These young people are inspirational. They let all of us know that there is still a promise for the future.

If we could but distill their essence, we might learn what it is that motivates our young people to stay on a positive course in spite of howling winds that would wreck their lives. We might be able to find the key to motivating a whole generation towards excellence and service. As you read, you will hear the voice of committed young people who yearn to step up and make a difference in the world.

We change lives,

We change minds,

We change the world,

One person at a time,

Through the Ron Brown Scholar Program.

History

Michael A. Mallory

President, CAP Charitable Foundation
Executive Director, Ron Brown Scholar Program

TEN YEARS AGO, THE CAP CHARITABLE
Foundation created the Ron Brown Scholar
Program, the only scholarship program of its kind
in existence today. As the first class of Ron
Brown Scholars was about to be selected, the
chairman of the foundation told me that this
would be no ordinary program. It would be
a community, a family of gifted intellectuals
whose size and breadth would be without
precedent. The Scholars, in turn, would provide
an invaluable base of support for each other,
allowing them to bring about social changes that
would otherwise be unobtainable. I was to
become their mentor, brother, father, confidant,
counselor, and friend. The journey that
began 10 years ago has been an exhilarating
and rewarding experience.

The Ron Brown Scholar Program annually awards
20 $40,000 college scholarships to extraordinary
African-American high school seniors. No
restrictions are placed on the students' choices of
school or discipline. Since 1997, the program
has awarded 181 scholarships, with Scholars
studying at colleges and universities across the
United States. Scholars' interests range from
medicine to public policy, from the creative arts to
business.

Competition for the 20 yearly slots is intense. The
number of applications has grown to more than
6,000 a year. Applications are reviewed at the program's headquarters in Charlottesville, Virginia,
by staff and a cadre of expert volunteers. After sur-
viving numerous rounds of screenings, 20 semi-
finalists are invited to Washington, D.C., for a
series of interviews with the Ron Brown Scholar
Selection Committee. Though the committee
reserves the right to award just 10 scholarships,
to date all 20 finalists each year have received
scholarship awards.

What distinguishes the Ron Brown Scholar
Program from other scholarship programs are not
only the selection criteria – a dedication to community service, a demonstration of leadership,
proven academic achievement, and financial
need – but also the degree of interconnectedness
it fosters between the Scholars.

The Scholars are afforded many opportunities,
including alumni mentorships and internships
with institutions ranging from the National
Institutes of Health to Goldman Sachs.

Most importantly, the program offers a sense of
pride and belonging to a group of exceptional
individuals dedicated to improving the quality
of life of the African-American community. One
unique way of keeping the group connected
is a triennial leadership conference, hosted by the
CAP Charitable Foundation for all Ron Brown

Scholars, at which guests of national and
international renown challenge the Scholars to
fulfill their individual and group potential. Two
conferences held in Aspen placed an emphasis
on leadership and career direction. In 2005,
the conference took place in the Berkshires and
focused on the arts, entertainment, and the media.

In 2001, as the first group of Ron Brown Scholars
graduated from college, the Ron Brown Scholar
Alumni Association (RBSAA) was formed.
That same year, the CAP Charitable Foundation
created the Council on African American Affairs,
a professionally-staffed center for thought
leadership based in Washington, D.C. The Ron
Brown Scholar Program, the RBSAA, and the
Council are integrally related. The Council was
created to provide a tangible way for Ron Brown
Scholars and Alumni to play an active role in
framing and debating critical public policy issues
that affect black Americans. In keeping with
the foundation's original vision, and the vision of
the Ron Brown Scholar Program, the Council
fulfills its mission by engaging the Scholars and
Alumni, along with community-based organizations and community members, to identify
relevant issues of concern to African Americans,
to conduct innovative research, and to develop
public policy recommendations that lead to
positive, measurable changes for black Americans.

It is our expectation that this family of Scholars
become a force that positively changes America.
Supportive, interactive, and unique, the Ron
Brown Scholar Program is beginning to make
an impact disproportionate to the number
of Scholars. It is a body of staggering intellect
that is growing by 20 each year.

I Have Risen

ESSAYS BY AFRICAN-AMERICAN YOUTH

Caprice Gray

New York, New York 2004

MY FATHER'S PEOPLE, WHO WERE LEFT ONLY the barren yellow dust of the plains and a mountain of memories to fill the great void, have a saying. *A man without a history* – and I can imagine now my grandmother telling me this, her gnarled spotted hands smoothing the patterns in her worn cotton skirt – *is like a wind in the buffalo grass.*

It has taken me seventeen years to find the truth in these words. My own yesterdays were, for a long time, unfortunate things I deemed better forgotten, left behind in the tired old dust of old apartments along with blackened pennies and worn crumbled photographs. I would shut the dark away and remember only the light: the soft warmth of my mother's embrace, the first patter of my baby sister's feet, the sound of laughter dodging through shafts of sun.

And yet I could not deny the existence of those dark times. They sometimes spilled out of tight cages in the farthest corners of my mind, smooth and slow and sinister, and I would remember. What got you through it, someone once asked me. My family, of course. My mother and little sisters, and my brother. And writing. Writing? Yes. Let me tell you . . .

From the time I was very young, and more accustomed to speaking to people's knees than their faces, I have written. *Girl-Who-Sculpts-Life-From-Ink,* I called myself, *Brown Bardess of the Barrio.* I wrote from the wind-tossed plain of black-tarred rooftops, from the shadow-soaked recesses of my bedroom closet. Writing was a way to escape, to free myself from that familiar choke-hold so endemic to the crumbling inner-city tenement building, to fly from the crushing cage of bare blank walls and scuffed linoleum, past the long prison-like hallways lit by dying yellow bulbs, and out of shadowed, dank stairwells steeped in the tangled odor of sweat and sin and stale, sleepy sad.

"Oh, mi niña," my next-door neighbor used to laugh, holding my face between soft warm palms that smelled of cheap flowered soap and *bodega* cigarettes, "always with the head in the clouds."

In the clouds, wrapped in a whispering white, I did not have to remember my father's hands circling hard around my mother's smooth, dark throat in the shadows of our tight-walled apartment, or her blood blooming crimson on our brown wood floors. There, I could forget that I was the little girl squatting against the wall and shuddering like a leaf in a December wind, tears making hot swift tracks down my cheeks (*"Stop, daddy."*) I could forget the sharp, sickening crunch of her bones breaking swift beneath his fist (*"No, daddy,"*) and the soft sounds of crying on cloud-strewn days. I could forget the hunger that seemed to fold the two sides of my stomach together sometimes when the welfare check ran out and the kitchen shelves sat smooth and empty and the refrigerator hummed its hollowness.

"That which doesn't kill you," my mother always sang with a softness in her eyes, "only makes you stronger."

It was my pen that turned my mourning into song when my sweet-faced cousin was murdered and left to leak his life out on the ice-laced streets of the Baltimore inner city, staining the frozen gutters that deep color of roses we never saw bloom.

It was my pen that shuddered when my father slipped into a coma one night from which long-faced doctors feared he would not return. And it was my pen that helped me endure the harsh reality of homelessness, cold winter evening pressed tight against a sea of brown bodies on the pale linoleum tiles of a colorless cafeteria, eating stiff leftover prison food and looking towards tomorrow.

Hovering over my shoulders like a dark rain-laden cloud, this was the history that I once wanted to fold away and forget. But I now know it is that very history that has made me stronger, that has molded me into what I am today.

A man without a history is like a wind in the buffalo grass, my grandmother whispers from Paha Sapa, the Black Hills. *You are more than the unseen, my child, more than an insubstantial rustle in the sun-warmed grass.* Rivers of light run through her hair and her woods spiral from thin old woman lips to weave amongst the stars. *You are the phoenix that has survived the flames and has become more beautiful because of it.*

Caprice Gray
New York, New York 2005

Caprice is a student at Yale University, where she plans to major in psychology. Writing continues to play an important role in her life.

Kelly L. Lee

Springfield, Oregon 2003

MANY A WISE MAN HAS SAID THAT ONE MUST acknowledge his faults before attempting to mend his flaws. So, I willingly place my innards on the table: I am a racist. I am a bigot. I let physical appearances distort my views of others. I allow ethnicity to influence my judgment.

I not only claim these defects for myself; I also ascribe them to the general public.

As an African American, I realize more than many how deeply racism is imbedded in society, in the human psyche. I have encountered prejudice in nearly every facet of my life. I've found that racism lies not only in the spoken word or vicious act, but also in perception. Racial slurs and hate crimes are simply the film that rests upon a foundation of tainted thought; the hatred that was alive and well 40 years ago is still around, clinging to society like withering ivy on an old stone wall.

Accepting unconcealed acts of racism as the beginning and end of hatred is easy. Verifying the subconscious existence of racism, however, is more difficult because it involves admitting personal guilt. Again, I offer the idea that *we* are not innocent.

Our perceptions of other people are governed by physical appearance. Think: we may not admittedly believe that Asians are smart, blacks are uneducated, and whites are business savvy, yet we are not surprised when Asians are at the top of the class, blacks are at the bottom of the social ladder, and whites are in fancy suits. But if we see an Asian thumbing through a dumpster we take notice; if we see an African American in Armani we look twice.

Our unconscious application of biases indicates that our prejudices have not burned out entirely. Hatred has, instead, crawled deep into the closets of our minds, further fogging the rose-colored lenses with which we judge society. When a black man was a "nigger," we found in racism a recognizable villain. Now that our racism is more frequently practiced than spoken, we do not notice race divisions as easily. Thus, we incorrectly believe that the problem of racism is not as serious as it once was.

As an individual who is often on the receiving end of racist thought, I live by the belief that all men are equal, and that many of humanity's greatest problems rise from inequality. I realize that our prejudices have an immeasurable effect on the ways society functions. Standards and expectations based on race act as new glass ceilings, hindering opportunities for advancement. Disputes between and within races inhibit effective community action and improvement. We cannot fight racism by addressing outbursts, because outbursts are the symptom of racist thought, not the causes. We must, instead, address the prejudice that festers within ourselves.

I dare say that, because of some perversion of *learned* nature, we will be racist as long as we have eyes to see gradation in skin tones and ears to hear differences in dialect. Because we are neither wholly blind nor deaf, we must attempt to reverse our bigotry. We can curb racism only if we consciously try to change ourselves.

Kelly L. Lee
Boston, Massachusetts 2005

Kelly studies sociology and Afro-American studies at Harvard University. She plans on completing a doctoral program in a field related to racial and class equity and identity formation.

Julian Miller

Winstonville, Mississippi 2003

"BABY, I WANT YOU TO GO ON TO MSMS AND do us all proud like I know you can do. Now, I know you love your old grandma, but I don't want you to worry about me, 'cause whatever happens to me rests in the capable hands of the Lord. Ever since you were born, I have worked hard to see this day . . . to see you go on to a better life and become a young man by taking hold of your future and getting a good education. And son, the only way you can disappoint me is not by leaving me, but by letting my hard work go up in smoke."

AT THAT VERY moment, I tearfully embraced my grandmother. I didn't say a word; I just cried like a baby and held her as tight as I could. On that day, I developed a whole new level of love and respect for my grandmother. My grandmother had just helped me make one of the most difficult decisions I had ever had to make: To leave home to attend the Mississippi School for Mathematics & Science. Actually, she practically took the decision out of my hands and made it for me.

The reason I was so worried about leaving home was the worsening of my grandmother's physical condition. I was concerned about who would take care of her in the wake of her failing health. I remember agonizing over the decision for tiresome days and sleepless nights. And in one unforgettable moment, the love, wisdom, and altruism of an extraordinary old lady prevailed over any doubts. On that day, I not only decided to attend MSMS, but I also gained invaluable insight into the importance of education – not only in my future, but the future of all African Americans.

From that moment on, I realized that education is the sole enzyme that will catalyze the journey of all African Americans through the 21st Century. Education is the key to survival. It is like the air we breathe. Like the sun, it gives us sustenance and warmth, and like the moon, it provides a beacon of hope through the dark path that is our reality in America.

Education encompasses all of the problems that we as a people *must* face as we enter the 21st Century. If African Americans would take advantage of every available school- and career-related opportunity, more of us would be strong providers rather than lay entities in America's economy. If African Americans would become more enlightened about the importance of abstinence, the AIDS epidemic would not plague our people as severely as it does. And if African Americans would realize that we all still have the same common goals and aspirations even though as individuals we may be very different, we as a people could embrace our brotherhood and finally end our long and arduous journey to the "Promised Land."

All this I realized thanks to my grandmother, a woman who received no formal education of her own, yet understood the life-changing impact it would have on me. She was well aware of the fact that the knowledge I would gain would contribute to my growth as an individual and empower me to accomplish anything I wanted. At the time, it seemed ironic to me that an uneducated woman could comprehend the significance of getting a good education, but I guess the hardship she endured as a result of her lack of education made her an expert on the subject.

Julian Miller
New York, New York 2005

*Julian studies government at Harvard University.
He took some time off during the 2005–06 school
year to help his grandmother recover from surgery.
She remains his inspiration.*

Brandon L. Nicholson

Oakland, California 2001

THE EASTMONT BARBER SHOP IS NOTHING like Locks & Lollipops Hair Salon. Eastmont is located deep in East Oakland, on 73rd and Foothill, a predominantly low-income, black and Latino urban neighborhood. Locks & Lollipops is one block away from my high school, Marin Academy (MA), located in a predominantly white, upper-income suburb.

Sports are central to the operation of Eastmont. The walls of the shop are covered with sports pennants, as well as the occasional risqué poster of swimsuit models. A television is positioned directly across from the cutting chairs so that each of the three barbers, D, Saleem, and Mr. D, can prepare for the constant debates that fill the shop with the sounds of black men, with their deep voices, squawking like eagles about which athlete had the most *juice*, or the most *flash*, or the most *game*.

These verbal contests are not always limited to sports; just as often they involve politics, cars, entertainment, and night clubs. Both patrons and barbers actively engage in these conversations. I love to just sit back and observe this interaction, so unrestrained and genuine. It is characteristic of my people to just get plain rowdy, to not care about proper etiquette or being penalized for saying exactly what's on their minds. There is an element in this shop that is closer to what I grew up with. It is like family there.

On the other hand, expressions spoken at the Marin Academy, where I spend most of my days, are unlike those made at the barber shop, uncensored and blurted out.

I have been making the approximately one-hour commute to MA from Oakland for four years now. MA is an institution that offers unlimited resources and opportunities. Students here engage in highly intellectual and academic colloquies. That's not to say that students at MA do not act like average teenagers, but discussions and activities here are much more controlled and calculated than at the shop.

I have made great efforts to be a part of the MA community. I always make a point of attending various athletic and admissions events; I serve on numerous committees, and I am president of the student body. Being submerged in MA's culture, in order to assimilate I could have chosen to discard any of my own cultural customs that I value. Instead, I have managed to maintain a balance. Both the school and the shop have facilitated something that is very culturally important to me: I can be who I am. I can be black in both places. I have the great fortune of experiencing the cultures of both Marin County and Oakland, and it makes sense for me to connect with both so I can fully appreciate them.

I am bicultural; I comfortably socialize with my white friends, and also go home and feel comfortable interacting with my black friends.

Hairstyle has always been a significant aspect of black teen life. I remember how some kids were ostracized because of their less-than-satisfactory haircuts.

However, it wasn't just the hairstyle that was important to so many black males; it was the experience behind the style – the *going to* the barber shop. For many of my peers, going to the shop was a cultural privilege; it was a bastion of black male camaraderie that provided an opportunity to discuss current events and life issues, and a place to grow.

There is a process called *lining up*, where the barber sharpens and cleans up the hairline. Every two weeks, regardless of what is going on, I just *have* to get lined up. In effect, when I do this I am also lining up my life with my culture to create balance. When I walk out of the shop after being lined up, I leave with a strong feeling of pride.

So, every two weeks I take a number and usually spend about two hours waiting at the shop. I don't think this happens at Locks & Lollipops. No one in Eastmont ever complains about how long he has to wait. They just sit there squawking, and, everybody knows, if you can't squawk you won't get recognized. I don't mind waiting. I just soak it all up, hoping they'll wait just a little longer to call my number.

Brandon L. Nicholson
Oakland, California 2005

*Brandon graduated from the Woodrow Wilson School
of Public and International Affairs at Princeton
University, where he concentrated in educational
policy. He is pursuing a Ph.D. in the same field
at the University of California, Berkeley.
He still gets lined up at the Eastmont Barber Shop.*

Nakiya K. Jones

Dallas, Texas 1999

I HATE CHICKEN. I'M NOT TALKING ABOUT a mild, temporary dislike attributed to finicky taste buds or the occasional mispreparation. No, this hate has blossomed into an unavoidable disgust. If it were up to me, every single "Why-did-the-chicken-cross-the-road?" joke would end in some grotesque form of poultrycide. This fowl-loathing did not develop overnight. It was a gradual cultivation, from supper after supper of chicken dumplings, chicken legs, fried chicken, broiled chicken, boiled chicken, chicken pot pies, etc. Since chicken is relatively cheap, and my family's monthly income was less than the average person's weekly, chicken was our staple.

But if this lack of material goods gave me more than an overwhelming repulsion for poultry, it also gave me motivation to attempt a better life.

To understand why overcoming poverty is such an amazing feat, one must first understand what poverty is.

Poverty is not attending my National Honor Society induction because my family did not have transportation to or appropriate clothing for the event. Poverty became a virtual albatross around my neck at speech and debate competitions. Imagine all of the debaters, donned in their double-breasted dark suits, carrying briefcases that cost more than my entire outfit, looking like little litigates-in-training, and there I stood, wearing the same polyester white shirt and black skirt I had worn to every previous competition. Despite the snickers and name-calling, I had the last laugh when the first place medals were placed around my K-Mart-collared shirt.

Poverty is developing the audacity to question God about the existence of the poor. Is it the luck of the draw that allows me to wear shoes while someone else goes without the privilege? Providence or probability, it is sickening to be confronted by the contorted face of poverty on a daily basis. In a household that struggles to keep warm plates of food on the dining room table, money for application fees and senior class rings does not take priority. Poverty is thanking God for chicken, even though you detest it, because there are others who are not granted the opportunity to buy it.

Yet, despite sub-human living conditions, a nomadic lifestyle, and constantly "going without," I have still managed to maintain an A average at each of the four high schools I have attended. In this respect, one can say that poverty can be used as a propeller for advancement. One of the reasons I spend two to four hours nightly doing homework, why I attend unneeded tutoring sessions and attempt unassigned Calculus problems is so that I will not have to stretch money all of my life.

I have already decided that with my first paycheck I am going to have lunch at one of the most expensive restaurants in town. And I will not be ordering the chicken.

Nakiya K. Jones
Los Angeles, California 2005

Nakiya studied journalism and political science at the University of Texas at Austin. She works for ACORN, a national non-profit organization in Oakland, California, where she manages grassroots political campaigns that benefit working-class communities of color. The day she got her first paycheck, she was coordinating volunteers for a grassroots event, and did not have time to cash it. She ended up eating box lunch leftovers, and you can guess what they were. She says she still eats chicken, but sparingly.

Delbert A. Green II

Opelousas, Lousiana 2004

OUTSIDE, IT'S THIS BRILLIANT LITTLE WHITE house, trimmed in that bold forest green, including the ramp of the same color that leads to an inviting front door. Inside, it's just as modest: three bedrooms and one bath, chipped floors and effulgent walls of mustard yellow. Fifty years ago, after contracting a cousin to build the house, my grandmother and her seven children moved into their new home. Since my grandmother's death, my mother, sister, and I have called it home.

Surrounding this house is the world I knew for the first sixteen years of my life. Situated in the heart of one of the most dangerous areas of the city, my house has seen its share of dire situations and been in the presence of terrible tragedy. Drugs, guns, and sex were in my backyard.

But every aspect of my being originates in this place. My sense of responsibility, my sense of humor, my compassion, and sense of fear all stem from events that I have endured here. In this house my dreams have grown – from the hope of learning to drive a car, to aspirations of attending a research university where I can best realize my passion and potential for science. I have transmogrified.

Last year, I only spent about eight weeks there. In addition to switching to the Louisiana School, a boarding school in Louisiana, I presented my research at three conferences. I got to sense life in "the big city" (Boston), see the beautiful sunrise across the Atlantic in Maine, and experience just why Cleveland rocks. During the summer, we traveled to Mt. Washington in New Hampshire; I remember looking out at one of the most amazing sights of my life.

But I never forgot home.

Each time I return home, turning onto Bossier St. and seeing the rosebush at the entrance to the door, a grin escapes me. I think about the times when Meghan, my sister, my cousin Edward, and I would explore the Amazon rainforest – a small backyard that during the day was merely scattered with trees and shrubs, but at night was an adventure. I remember the "Funky Fresh Kids," the musical groups we created, and the songs we sang. Also resounding in my mind is the time when a huge dog chased us onto my mother's car, and the time we heard what we thought was a firecracker, which actually was a gunshot.

I consider myself very lucky for being blessed not only with my abilities, but also the courage to pursue them. And it is my nurturing in Opelousas that gave me this attitude. As I acquire more opportunities to explore my love for science, taking me further from home, I push myself to pursue these new worlds, not to escape the old, but to grow immune to the bounds imposed on those who came before me.

Delbert A. Green II
Glenarden, Maryland 2005

*Delbert studies biology and biological engineering
at the Massachusetts Institute of Technology.
He would like to establish a lab to work alongside the
World Health Organization to study the science
of infectious diseases. He still goes home to Opelousas
whenever he gets the chance.*

Wendy F. Francois

Naranja, Florida 2003

RIGHT NOW I FEEL LIKE A BIRD CAGED without a key, yet I know why the caged bird sings. My parents often stop and stare at me with joy and revelry; I am first generation, first American, first hope. Simultaneously, they surreptitiously impress the "back home customs" upon me, a tactic that is used to keep me from flying.

I was raised to understand that, in Haiti, a young girl serves her parents, lives to please them, and remains with them until marriage. Back home, young girls wear uniforms to school. They cook and they hand-wash their clothes just as their matriarchs do. They do not wear skirts above their knees. They do not casually converse with boys on the phone. They do *not* look elders in the eye.

I, on the other hand, am quite different, but I cannot deny the brand of my culture on my character. Many Haitians have few possessions and receive little respect. Humility is among their possessions as is self-respect. Whenever the accolades begin to accumulate, I quickly remember where I came from. Detractors are defied, because I do not compromise the discipline that I have acquired by indulging in vengeful retorts. I am headstrong and believe in the relentless pursuit of my goals rather than parental approval of them. I am driven by the obligation to excel in my strengths through higher learning and to utilize them to benefit the advancement of all of society, not just those who share my roots. Higher learning presupposes change – change of ideology, change of concerns, change of location. I am not afraid of change; I welcome it. The pursuit of higher education away from home is essential to my growth and the sophistication of my character.

That's why I say that I know why the caged bird sings; singing is the key to her freedom. She's so rare and beautiful to others, but she has more to offer than her beauty. I am like this caged bird because my cultural mores threaten to clip my wings. My parents love me and admire my achievements, but they were not fortunate enough to experience higher learning. They fear the unknown and, consequently, fetter my ambition. My parents escaped the perils of Haiti on a rickety raft amid 100 other refugees seeking streets paved with gold.

The caged bird hypnotizes its crowds by crooning lovely melodies. Similarly, I rip through deterrent currents and excel academically – in spite of turbulence – because my education is the key to my freedom. Without it, I can't fly. My education is my dream; indeed, it is the essence of my life. With an opportunity to spread my wings I will not only fly, but soar. I will fulfill my dreams of becoming a medical doctor. Ever reminiscent of my parents' perilous voyage, I will save and improve lives.

Many people say, "The sky's the limit." To me there are no limits. There is the whole world to see, and there is much beyond the sky.

Wendy F. Francois
New York, New York 2005

*Wendy studies political science and human rights
at Columbia University and plans to become
a medical doctor.*

Morgan K. Dooley

Atlanta, Georgia 1999

I AM THE PRESIDENT OF THE B.E. MAYS TEEN Aquatic Club, the only scuba diving club in the nation, maybe the world, comprised entirely of African-American teenagers. We have already completed well over twenty dives, raised thousands of dollars, and probably have the largest operating cost of any club at my high school. In addition to braving the risk of drowning every time we make a dive, we also chance air embolisms (the rupturing of the lungs) and nitrogen narcosis (a narcotic condition resulting from over-exposure to pressurized nitrogen). So, am I crazy for being a scuba diver?

There are certainly people who think so. Yet, what I tell them is this: Scuba diving is something that sets me apart. Not everybody has what it takes to be a diver. Of the forty people who signed up for the class with me that day, only twelve of us were actually certified. Diving isn't just a recreation; it is a passion. I compare it to being in the armed forces; it just becomes a way of life. Scuba diving has reinforced my best qualities – discipline and hard work – and has helped me to develop qualities I never even knew that I had – leadership and patience, for example.

Especially as an African American, being a scuba diver has led me to many experiences that I wouldn't have otherwise had. One of the most meaningful experiences of my life occurred on a dive trip. Off the coast of Florida, near Key Largo, about thirty feet down in the Atlantic Ocean, lies the wreck of the "Ivory," a slave ship that crashed on a coral reef in 1850. When the "Ivory" sank, so did all on board – including all of the Africans chained in the cargo hold, bound for slavery in the United States.

We made an initial trip to the wreck in 1997, but we knew that we wanted to do more. Through doughnut sales and sponsorships, the dive club was able to raise enough money to create a bronze statue in honor of the black men and women who died on that ship. The statue, designed and created by an art teacher at my school, bore the names of all of the members of the B.E. Mays Teen Aquatic Club. We finally made that second trip to the wreck in February of 1998, to deliver the statue. It was an absolutely life-changing experience. To be so close to such a tangible piece of my history as an African American was stunning.

Right before we lowered the memorial on to the wreckage, I said a prayer. It included a Yoruba proverb that essentially summed up how we all felt at that moment. It says, "If we stand tall, it is because we stand on the backs of those who came before us. . . ."

Morgan K. Dooley
Atlanta, Georgia 2005

Morgan received a bachelor's degree in anthropology and human biology from Emory University in 2003, and an MPH in global health from the Rollins School of Public Health in 2005. She is now a medical *student at Johns Hopkins University in Baltimore. She still loves to dive, but it's become an expensive hobby for her student lifestyle.*

Lindsay Lally Cothrine

Bolingbrook, Illinois 2005

I HAVE NO IDEA WHAT TO WRITE. IT'S SICK. I've spent my whole life dreaming of becoming some vision of academic perfection, some scholastic goddess that the educated bow to in awe . . . Then it all comes down to an essay.

What is my personal statement? What do I want to do with my life? Why are we here? Oddly enough, I have answers for the last two, but sadly, I can say no single definite thing of myself.

I've been called original, a perfectionist, and on my cell phone during church. I recognize no box to think out of, no glass full or empty, or margins for error. I think that optimism is for wishers, not doers. Pessimists are equally lazy.

I am not bitter, I am cynically hopeful. I am not condescending, I just have high standards.

I believe in the power of change. I believe in the U.S. government system. I believe that, in case of doubt, lie and sound convincing.

I think that everyone during their lifetime should put their whole being into something, and fail. I am dreading that failure.

I speak semi-fluent German, I think Spanish is boring, and often rant in Yiddish.

I admit to knowing the lyrics to "Tiny Dancer."

I believe that there is a fine line between "hobby" and "mental illness." That said, I am a very sick person.

I enjoy sports. I am a blocker in volleyball, a forward in basketball, and a MVP in softball. I throw discus in track. I often jump to conclusions.

I am a pacifist, an activist, and a free spirit. I think everyone should follow their dreams – unless it's the one where they go to school naked.

I defend animals, the homeless, and anyone who is being treated unjustly. Ironically, some people find my defensive stance offensive.

It worries me that only the good die young.

I have seen that a journey of a thousand miles begins with a single step. I know now that the strength of that journey comes from the fellow travelers you meet along the way.

All in all, I do not know who I am – not exactly. Most seventeen-year-olds don't. But I do know what I stand for, I know what I'd fall for, and I know what I believe in, and at the end of the day, I think that's all that matters.

Lindsay Lally Cothrine
Naperville, Illinois 2005

Lindsay is a freshman at Yale University, where she plans to pursue a joint ethics, politics and economics major.

Kareemah Love Sabur

Buffalo, New York 2004

THEY ARE SCIENCE'S HARDCORE REBELS. They refuse to follow the conventions of normalcy, and they stubbornly stay in places they're not wanted. They have a most infamous reputation among scientists, and nearly everyone describes them as tough and relentless. After years of working with cancer cells, I respect them.

The treatment/research nature of the Roswell Park Institute provides me constant reminders of my ultimate goal as a researcher: the acquisition of knowledge for both the prevention of and the cure for the disease. But after care-taking for these cells, I have acquired an appreciation for their non-conformist attitude. Normal pathway models and paradigms don't apply, and one finding often leads to a thousand new questions.

Part of the motivation for beginning my research has been the alarming increase in the incidence of breast cancer among American women. I was also extremely concerned with the sharp contrast of prognosis in the lower-income African-American community as compared with others. Hoping to pursue a career in medicine, I have also sought in my research a better understanding of the molecular aspects of the body. The widespread and diverse nature of cancer makes it both a global concern in and of itself and an indirect window into many other branches of medicine relating to other types of diseases. This added dimension of diversity gives cancer cells an advantage in resisting most attempts to control or destroy them. The challenge of working with such an unpredictable bunch excites me and makes my laboratory work something more than just peering through microscopes at petri dishes.

The desire to help those in need played an undeniable role in my choice to be a researcher. In the same breath, the connection I feel with the laboratory atmosphere and the cells themselves has maintained my initial zest for the challenges involved. Of all my activities, this one has surprisingly become my most beloved.

I have encountered people whose passion and excitement are nothing short of electrifying.

Observing scientists within the institute convinced me this was something I wanted to be a part of. This disease has been able to do something that, in all of our crusades and killing, we have failed to do: to sit the rabbi next to the preacher, the Arab next to the American, to open the ears of the old to the voices of the young. We all share a bond that centers on these tiny organisms. The statistics cannot lie: cancer cells have robbed us of many lives, but the true loss occurs if we ignore the lessons they offer.

The world has come to know cancer as almost an immortal enemy. If we are ever to truly defeat cancer in all its forms, I'm sure we'll have to include some ingenious tactics. In that respect, I think we can learn something from these elusive little foes. Cancer cells have no problem working in unfamiliar territory, or trail-blazing. So, as my eyes stare at the cells under the microscope, I see something that I admire, and that has the potential to change the thinking of the human race in more than one way.

Kareemah Love Sabur
Cambridge, Massachusetts 2005

Kareemah is studying biology at Harvard University.
She still plans on becoming a medical researcher.

Immanuel R. Foster

Berkeley, California 2002

HIDDEN IN A DOWNTOWN OAKLAND ALLEY-WAY is the Will Rogers Hotel.

Mice, rats, roaches, bacteria, and downtrodden people have colonized the Will Rogers. Its prison-cell-sized rooms house whole families. Human feces are smeared on the shower walls of its communal bathrooms. An aggregate stench of rot, urine, alcohol, and vomit permeates the hallways. There are crying beeps from smoke detectors with dying batteries, shouting crack addicts, louder-shouting crack dealers, cigarette burns on the carpets, peeling paint, barred windows, a malfunctioning elevator, and creaking stairs.

The Will Rogers Hotel is the place where I first became conscious of critical choices I would have to make in my life and of the actions I would take to implement them.

During my thirteenth and fourteenth years, the Will Rogers was my home and the home of other people forgotten by society, the people on skid row, people like my mother. She worked the graveyard waitress shift at Denny's, while my father was out somewhere "giving my mother space" and dealing with his depression.

I was almost always home alone, free to mingle with the other hotel residents. I used to love having conversations with them. They were all battling their own problems: cop problems, drug problems, alcohol problems, social problems, money problems, marital problems, and so on. And they unburdened themselves with me. Their life stories and anecdotes intrigued me with their enormous variety. Almost every day I learned something new about life. I suppose you could say that they were my bedtime stories.

They also taught me survival strategies: "When you sell crack, you hide it under your tongue so that when the five-O come you can swallow it and get it back when you shit it out later." I had never thought about selling crack, and I quickly decided that I never wanted to.

Maybe it was because of all the stories I heard at the Will Rogers – and the many similar places I lived – that I started to do well in school. After all, there were good stories to be heard at school, too, and unlike the Will Rogers, where I could not ask questions, at school good questions were actually encouraged. Moreover, I enjoyed the predictability of the school day and the stability of the classroom environment. I was fascinated by what I was learning – topics so different from the lessons of my home.

Many of the people I knew at the Will Rogers were good people who had encountered difficulties they were not prepared to face –

difficulties that had broken them, making them lose hope for a better life. I empathized with my neighbors, but there was not much I, then 13, could do to help them. Seeing their situations strengthened my resolve to lead a different life. I chose to work hard at school because I knew that, by doing so, in the future I might actually be able to help them, or people like them.

As I started to achieve scholastically, I found myself making friends at school with a wider spectrum of people. White middle class kids, for example, invited me to their homes. The first time I walked into the house of one of my new friends I saw a clean carpet, pristine white walls, parquet floors, plump furniture, and his smiling mother in the spotless kitchen, preparing an after-school snack.

Before walking into that house I thought such lives existed only on television. During my first visits I felt uncomfortably self-conscious and didn't know how I was supposed to behave. After some time, however, this feeling vanished and was replaced by a heightened awareness of the way some children are brought up to succeed and others to fail. While I enjoyed my new friends, I knew that there were people back at the Will Rogers, my other companions, struggling to pay their rent. There were so many people who led disconnected lives – lives without love, warmth, or dignity. I even felt a sense of guilt because, through choice, tenacity, and perhaps a bit of luck, l was on a trajectory that would enable me to leave behind the world of the Will Rogers.

Eventually my family managed to find a publicly subsidized apartment in Berkeley, but I have never forgotten the Will Rogers. Since then, I have served food at homeless shelters and have sat and shared conversations with the people there, still benefiting from some of their reflections. I often stop on the street and converse with beggars; more than money, many of them merely want someone to talk to.

Meanwhile, I have become an assiduous student. I regularly stay up late reviewing chapters meticulously and making detailed notes. I have attended public lectures at UC Berkeley, and, through the Quest Scholars Program, private lectures at Harvard University. I know my studies will help me contribute to my community.

Prior to the Will Rogers Hotel I had lived in many low-income, violent environments; I had spent nights sleeping in the park with my sister, or by myself, when both my parents were in jail. Among these varied living situations, the Will Rogers will always be special for me as the place where, in the thirteenth and fourteenth years of my life, I became conscious of the pivotal choices I was making.

Immanuel R. Foster
Oakland, California 2005

Immanuel studies history and science at Harvard University and plans to go to law school. On his visits home, he still stops by the Will Rogers Hotel.

Katori Hall

Memphis, Tennessee 1999

"LOOK AT THAT GIRL . . .
She ain't nothin' but a OREO!"

The crowd burst into laughter as I walked past.
I huddled my books closer to my chest as the tears
streamed down my cocoa-colored face. As a
five-year old, I never understood why they called
me "the dirty white girl," an "Oreo," or a "wigger."
Was it because of my pale-skinned friends?
Was it my incessant use of grammatically correct
sentences? Or was it just the fact that I knew the
words to all of Garth Brook's songs?

I always wondered how one acted "black" or how
one acted "white." I struggled to define my
blackness for the greater part of my childhood.
Webster's labeled "black" as being gloomy, evil,
or even indicating disgrace. Infuriated, I refused
to let those words describe me. If I could write
a book to educate not only young African
Americans but all people, I would write about
the true meaning of blackness.

Though being in high-level classes has helped
me grow intellectually and mentally, I have had to
pay a price. Many of my African-American
peers have segregated me. Many times I have
heard the comments, "Katori, you're too smart for
me," or "You think you're too good for us."
These comments have left me confused and
angry. Just because I learn around white students
and have white friends does not mean I check
the "white" box on my college applications.
The only thing I have wanted was my black peers
to see me as a young woman trying hard to
get somewhere in life. I am merely continuing the
dream of my ancestors, who, in their lifetimes,
despite obstacles, persevered and accomplished
spectacular feats. I know that education and
hard work are vital to help me achieve my dreams,
and through my book I want to teach other
African Americans that they can use education
to achieve their dreams, too.

Not only do some of my black peers tend to
stereotype me, but many of my white peers do so
as well. They have said to me that the only
reason I am getting into a good college is because
I am black. They do not see the long hours I
have spent poring over my books, they do not see
my fight to keep up my grades, nor do they see
my struggle to be the best that I can be. They only
see that I am black. I want to teach them that
black people are smart, and given the chance, can
achieve anything.

Time and time again, I have sought to define
blackness. Unfortunately, blackness refuses to be
defined by mere words. Former African kings
and queens, slaves, and civil rights activists all
comprise the essence of blackness. Blackness
stands as the will to achieve, the will to persevere,
and the will to be strong. Blackness is the ability
to overcome obstacles, survive storms, and make
sacrifices. My book would educate the world
that blackness means all those things and a great
deal more, for I am that book. My forefathers
wrote the legacy, and with my pen I intend to add
to our goals, our achievements, and our lives.

Katori Hall
New York, New York 2005

Katori studied African-American studies and creative
writing at Columbia University. She graduated
with a Master's of Fine Arts in acting from Harvard
University. She is a published playwright and plans
on becoming an actor. She lives in New York City.

Brent E. Cash

Glenarden, Maryland 2004

BANG! I HEARD THE GUNSHOT, BUT WAS unsure if it was real or not. Thump! I saw the body crumble, but wondered if it really happened. Rather than hearing and seeing these atrocities for myself, I had heard the gunshot and seen the body vicariously, through a friend's story. Joseph was the victim. He saw a girl he liked, he asked for her phone number, and was consequently shot by someone else who liked the girl. Lately, he associated with the wrong crowd, but his actions that night did not merit death.

Joseph was a friend, someone that I guarded on the basketball court whenever we played. Chills crept down my spine; I could still feel his cold sweat splashing onto me when we struggled for the ball. And suddenly I could remember no more. There was a strange smell in the room. This time my senses were not imaginary, because the scent was definitely real. "Put that out!" I screamed at Daniel. He had finished his story on Joseph, but had started something else – smoking marijuana. He offered me some, but, to his disappointment, I scowled, narrowing my eyes into miniscule slants and snorting gruffly.

Such were the fates of my childhood friends. Unmotivated in school, either gang life or drugs took their toll on them. I ended communications with them and became an outsider to my neighbors, a stranger to longtime buddies. I knew my challenge was to remain focused in school. Highly motivated by the possibility of becoming the first four-year college student in my immediate family, and the only one within my group of "friends" to pursue higher education, learning became a passion. I devoted my energy to becoming a scholar, staying late at school to study in the library, participating in activities, and avoiding the neighborhood's negativity.

Yet, I was disheartened and unsatisfied; I had abandoned my "friends," and believed that they, too, should have the same opportunities that I did, no matter their horrible decisions.

Motivated to prevent kids from self-destructing, I instituted a tutoring program at the neighborhood elementary school designed to counter the evils that destroyed my friends. They had told themselves "I can't" too many times, even when they could; ultimately, they just gave up. My goal is to prevent this from happening to my students. "I can't do that math problem," a student told me. To his shock, I told him to come to the blackboard, and with a little help he finished the problem to perfection.

This program has inspired youngsters to realize their potential, a thought that makes me smile broadly because I know that they will not commit the same glaring mistakes as my childhood friends. The program, which has lifted my con- science, is a response to my old friends' decisions; it is my attempt to save others who, possibly, are like them. I am proud that I have played a part in shaping the futures of so many youngsters.

Brent E. Cash
Glenarden, Maryland 2005

*Brent studies mechanical engineering and economics
at Duke University. He still returns to his old
neighborhood, where his family continues to live.*

Preston Scott Copeland

Baltimore, Maryland 2004

WE OFTEN THINK THAT OUR CHARACTER IS determined by the ocean – not the drops. We think that people will remember us for the "life-changing" moments, those societal milestones that inspire grandiloquent toasts ("May the connubial union of Sharon and Bob luxuriate in a plethora of blissful years,") or heartrending confessions ("He cheated on me! Why did he do it! I shall never date again, Hortense!").

But I disagree. Miranda, in John Fowles' *The Collector,* was right: We humans are defined moment by moment, drop by drop. Our character is fashioned out of a trickle of small, never-ending decisions. And drops may seem insignificant until you consider that the huge stalagmites of the Luray Caverns in Virginia were formed from a few drops of limewater falling once or twice a year for eons.

As such, perhaps an investigation of some "drops" from a typical Preston morning may help reveal the ocean that is me.

Complication 1, 5:00 am: Strains from a Loreena McKennitt CD gradually assault my ears in ever-increasing volume. My CD-alarm clock is sounding. But my blue cotton sheets feel so warm, like a cocoon, and outside it's still dark. Will I get up or not?

Decision 1, 5:01 am: I do, in fact, get up on time. Some might say that it is a foregone conclusion, the non-decision of a boy who is required by state law to attend school. Oh, ye of little imagination. Others might realize that this is a significant existential act. Like Kierkegaard, I am taking a "leap into the darkness" of the world (literal darkness – after all, it's only 5:00 am,) affirming my will to exist. Despite the irrationality of a world devoid of meaning, I choose to wake up and fight!

Complication 2, 5:24 am: While I brush my teeth in the bathroom adjacent to her bedroom, my mother stirs. She really is a light sleeper. A muffled "Good morning" passes feebly through the white bedroom door. I could easily pretend I don't hear her; after all, I'm busy brushing my teeth. Do I take the time to spit out my toothpaste and greet her?

Decision 2, 5:24 am: I do. And this is a hassle, let me assure you. Rembrandt whitening toothpaste does not come cheap. But I bellow a hearty "Hello, Mom!" and exchange pleasantries for a few seconds. How Kantian of me to exercise the categorical imperative so early in the morning. But in this case, I *must* behave as if my actions create a principle that will determine the actions of everyone else. After all, what if all children didn't greet their mothers at dawn?

The mothers would become so disgruntled they would cease to care for us and go on a global strike. And since it is common knowledge that mothers actually run the world, controlling every member in the American government except Rumsfeld – that man eats nails for breakfast and was bred among wolves – lack of their support would result in global chaos. So, "Hello, Mom!" it is.

Complication 3, 6:20 am: I prepare a breakfast of soggy eggs, slimy bacon, and lemon twist V-8. As I sit down at the dining room table, Rand's *The Fountainhead* in hand, I think about her atheistic objectivist philosophy, which in many aspects I embrace. She would applaud my ambition to create, to do, to be in this world. She would scorn my desire to honor a God whose existence I can neither rationally prove nor refute. Rand is a genius, and one of my heroes. Do I dare buck her doctrine and say "Grace"?

Decision 3, 6:21 am: I pray before I eat. I must confess that this decision is more practical than philosophical. As perhaps was gleaned, I am not a good cook. Asking God to bless my comestibles is a matter of survival. I've had food poisoning before, and it's not exactly a gentle ride on the Tilt-A-Whirl. More like writhing in pain on the Mind Eraser. But still, I'm somewhat proud that I had the courage to combine branches of Christian existentialism with rigid objectivism. I'm an individual after all.

Take that, your so called "life-changing" moments. I've experienced a complete philosophical awakening, and it's not even time for school yet.

Preston Scott Copeland
Baltimore, Maryland 2005

Preston is studying at Harvard University,
planning to concentrate in German cultural studies
and linguistics.

Miya Nicole Cain

Miami, Florida 2004

IN MY SEMI-CONSCIOUS STATE, I FORCED my drowsy eyelids to open to the blurry haze of a sterile hospital room. Waves of pain radiated through my foot, and I cringed as the searing torment grew in intensity. Tears welled in my eyes as I grabbed my mom's hand, squeezing tightly enough to cut off her circulation. Writhing and squirming, I attempted to shake the painful demon from my foot, but I realized that my attempts were futile. My only option was to prop up the leg with the cast and wait for the pain-killers to work their magic.

When I woke from the fourth, and last, corrective surgery 12 years ago, I was sure it was going to be the last problem I would have due to the abnormality with which I was born – club feet. Little did I know that, by rearranging the bones in my ankles several times, doctors had restricted their movement so that, although my feet were no longer turned upside down, the pain would recur. Fortunately, a lengthy path of rehabilitation, strength, and determination has allowed me to experience a life full of opportunity and physical freedom.

Hobbling around school on crutches, I incurred a barrage of questions about what had happened and why I wore a cast. Still, in fact, anytime someone glimpses my railroad-track scars, they are inclined to inquire about their origins. I always attempt to live normally and erase my foot problem from my memory; nevertheless, difficulties seem to rise from below when they are most unwelcome.

"Point and flex, girls, point and flex!" The voice of my old ballet teacher echoed in my head as I struggled to perform the first, supposedly simple, exercise that began the class. "Miya," she scolded, "you're not pointing." Indignantly, I replied that I was pointing as far as my feet would go, but she would not hear of such a thing. Warm blood rose to my cheeks and humiliation overcame me as she made an example of me to the others. Why couldn't I point like the other girls in the class? Being ahead of everyone in school was useless to me now. Tirelessly, day after day, I strove to keep up with the class, but each time I returned to my home, the familiar flames of pain lacerated my feet. My podiatrist, my parents, and reluctantly, I myself, realized that, at the moment, dancing was not in the picture.

After being limited on several occasions by the stiffness of my ankles, I resolved to take some course of action. A couple of phone calls and appointments later, I had my very own orthotics, or braces, for my shoes. The doctor also gave me a long, red rubber cord for daily half-hour strengthening exercises, a grueling process that I began to dread. Nevertheless, I knew that every salty tear that stung my cheek, each bead of sweat that crawled down my forehead, was a soldier in the battle with the titans that stomped across my lower legs.

Years later, I was determined to have full ability of my ankles and feet: I would run, I would dance, I would fly. Joining the track team in eighth grade was a monumental step in my life, and completing the season successfully – despite having to wrap my ankles daily – inspired me the following year to join the cross country team. Every day, after five miles of a grueling run through the thick Miami air, I felt a profound sense of accomplishment: My feet could carry my weight. Unfortunately, during the night they became different entities. Throbbing pain permeated my muscles, at times forcing me to crawl through my house. But I refused to quit the team. Instead, tenacity steeled my resolve, and day in and day out I trained for the meets. "Don't cry, don't stop," I chanted once throughout an entire race. I was determined that I wouldn't quit, and that no one would have to feel sorry for me because of my feet.

By the end of the season, in spite of my peculiar predicament I actually became an important member of the team. I, who could never stand up the entire night of a carnival, I, whose legs had never imagined such distances, even scored points at the district meet. Although my doctor forbade me to run such lengths ever again due to the strain on my muscles, I now had something that no one could ever take away from me – pride, pride in the fact that mind could truly triumph over matter.

Occasionally, needles of venom still pierce my feet, but I have found anti-venom to dull the pain. Rather than cursing this dilemma as a disability, I praise it as a gift: I was blessed with the ability to rehabilitate my feet, as well as the power to overrule physical weakness with mental strength.

Miya Nicole Cain
New York, New York 2005

*Miya is completing her pre-med requirements and
majoring in cognitive science at Yale University.
She plans to go into medicine. Miya no longer runs,
but she loves to dance and do yoga in spite of the
pain she still endures.*

Ihotu J. Ali

Hopkins, Minnesota 2003

CLAIROL NEEDS MORE MOISTURIZER, Pantene Pro-V creates too much volume, and Herbal Essences smells lovely but it doesn't work. Biolage makes curls stiff and crunchy like prom hair, while Salon Selectives is simply not made for an African mane. I've tried the entire Frizz-Ease product line. No luck.

For the past 17 years I've experimented, quite possibly, with every cream, spray, gel, and foam ever created that claims to "smooth out frizzies," "energize for defined curls," or "keep flyaways away." Mine is a severe case, and I still search for a cure.

Some days are better than others, but on average my hair is best described as "poofy." It's a cross between cute-curly and you-need-a-hair-brush-frizzy, with a few tangles added in each morning, just for variety. I have painful memories of my poor mother trying to tackle the unruly frizz-curls with only a wooden-handled brush. It may seem sturdy, but do not be fooled. We should've been using a machete.

For years I studied other girls' hair – long and blond, shimmering in the sun, or silky brown, dangling in front of the eyes. I hated my hair for not bouncing while I walked, and how snarls always caught my fingers when I tried to run them straight through. So every morning I tucked away my wild and tangled frizziness in tight buns, trying to blend in among the blonde and brunette beauties.

At school, I watched the actions and personalities of my classmates. What if I couldn't play like the kids on the playground? What if the girl sitting next to me in math class wouldn't smile back? So I stayed quiet. My frizz-curls, hidden in that bun, stayed quiet too.

My parents divorced before I entered junior high, causing the first of several moves for my mother, sisters, and me. Trying to release more of my identity with each new school, I gradually let my hair out of its bun – at first just on Halloween, so I could call it a costume, then again for the following Valentine's Day party. Eventually it made regular appearances at school dances as well. The less I wished for the hair and personalities of others, the more I began to see a new kind of beauty in myself – a beauty that had been concealed within tightly-wound knots, blurred by wispy flyaways, and smothered by fear of being different.

Today, my hair is free and rests on my shoulders, as it did yesterday and will do tomorrow. I cannot run my fingers straight through, nor will it ever bounce with my every step. Likewise, I will never act exactly like my peers; I laugh a little too loudly, and devote myself a little too deeply. My favorite Friday night activities include star-spinning and karaoke-singing, or simply settling in to the insights of a wise author. I have goose-bump moments while listening to great choral music, and I find equal excitement in discovering symbolism or literary devices in a poem. My greatest aspirations lie not in wealth or fame, but in loving more than I am loved, living with integrity and faith, and awaking each morning knowing that there could never be another head of frizz-curls exactly like mine.

Ihotu J. Ali
Hopkins, Minnesota 2005

*Ihotu is studying international studies and
political science, with a focus on Africa,
at Macalester College.*

Jessica Larché

Gretna, Louisiana 2003

THE WIND WAS UNUSUALLY CALM ON THAT humid Christmas Eve night, as is typical in the New Orleans area. Jennifer Larché struggled to rise from her comfortable seat in the hospital's waiting room to go for one of her last check-ups before the expected birth of her child.

Up to this point, life had not been easy for the thirty-year-old accountant who was struggling to maintain her career and pregnancy. Her husband, recently jailed for armed robbery and drug possession, abandoned her when she was four months pregnant. Yet, this little token left from their love, this little piece of him that resided in her, gave her hope for a new beginning.

Jennifer did not expect her baby until New Year's Eve, but born to the unsuspecting woman at 6:56 pm on that Dec. 24, 1984, was me, Jessica Noel Larché.

When I was a child, my mother and I struggled fiercely with financial hardship, resulting in the use of food stamps to keep us both fed. I remember the late night phone calls, every blue moon, from my incarcerated father. My mother, in an attempt to stay strong, continually encouraged me to love my father; she hid his situation from me in order to not affect my love and affection for him. Fortunately, I had my grandfather who served dutifully in my father's place. With guidance from these two wonderful role models, I pursued my academic success and became a local celebrity for my work in community commercials.

At the age of nine I met my father, and for the first time I was able to match the voice on the phone with a face that resembled mine. I could not have been happier, yet an impediment in my happiness came when my beloved grandfather died. His death gave me a new perspective on life. It taught me the true meaning of *carpe diem,* a lesson I will not soon forget.

As quoted from Ralph Ellison's *Invisible Man,* "The truth is the light and the light is the truth."

For me, Howard University is that distant light – the light of hope and success, the light that burns so brightly in the middle of this dark era.

Every generation has its own perils, but my generation seems to be afflicted by self-imposed plagues. I envision myself as the one who will eradicate the ignorance and illness that pervade my generation. In my school, people often refer to me as "the smart girl," or the president of student council, but the title that becomes me most is friend. That is what I will become to all Americans – a shoulder to cry on as we press forward out of darkness.

In Ralph Ellison's *Invisible Man,* the narrator realizes that for most of his life he was invisible, but at the end he challenges us to discover our own individuality. I feel that Howard University will help me confirm my individuality, and it is important to the future of our people and our nation that a foundation at Howard be my future so we may become visible.

Each of the adversities I have encountered, whether due to race, financial trouble, or lack of a conventional family, is an ingredient of the conglomeration that makes me who I am. Despite these setbacks, I have been blessed with the top ranking in my senior class and several academic and community leadership positions. I consider myself to be the anti-stereotype, for I have risen above low expectations and exceeded my wildest dreams.

So, this is an unfinished story, searching for its ending. . . .

Jessica Larché
Tallahassee, Florida 2005

Jessica studies political science and broadcast journalism at Florida A&M University.

Dorothy Loretta Ann Smith

Dallas, Texas 1999

EVERY DAY ON THE WAY HOME FROM SCHOOL, as I drive down Walnut Hill I notice, on my right, this graffiti-covered wall. Gang signs drawn in dark blood-red or deep black decorate this wall. The shaded outlines of past writings that can't be erased creep in the corners, symbols of power to be respected. Yet what *I* see is a wall soiled with the dirt of ignorance and covered with images of destruction. It is the same wall – just two different meanings.

I turn the corner into Webb Chapel, nearing the bus stop where usually a group of young men or women stand joking around. Here, joking around sometimes takes on a new meaning. I hear curse words and the N-word roll off the tongues of these so-called friends. Most do not even know the stereotypes they are creating at that bus stop. "Ignorant" and "violent" is what we hear on the news and read in the papers. Yet I know that their minds are full of the knowledge of survival and the games of life, their hearts full of fire and pride. Maybe they do not know the significance of the struggle to replace these stereotypes with respect. Instead of using their energy for positive effects, they hurt each other.

Farther down this street, I see the man in the wheelchair, his eyes lined with red veins, swollen and sunk deep into his face. His clothes, sweat-soaked and torn, hang on his body. He is always there, sometimes a paper bag-covered bottle in his lap. He never asks for anything, which makes it easier to ignore him. But he is there – a part of the neighborhood, a reminder of what could happen if one gives up.

How many more members of this society have resigned themselves to destruction because they do not know any better, they do not think they can do better, or they are tired of trying to break out of the trap of poverty or failure? Why is there no one to give them a chance? Millions of charity organizations, thousands of shelters and soup kitchens, and hundreds of programs are designed to rehabilitate the "misfits" of society. Yet, people still stand on the corners of the freeway with "need help" signs. Young people kill each other, trying to be the toughest, because that is the only way to gain the power and identity they so desperately yearn for.

This is what I want to change. I want to bring hope, a word with a meaning so deep as to change one's entire life.

Changing the wrongs of society is my dream. It may be idealistic, but it's a task I plan to take on piece by piece. Community service has become a significant part of my life. It has allowed me to develop compassion – instead of pity – for those in need. As a young woman, I've already seen the effects of people who don't care, of a society that offers limited options. Problems are denied, facts ignored. The reality is that many people think they have no choices, and I can't ignore that reality because it's in my neighborhood.

As a member of society, it's my duty to take care of my neighbors. One person can only do so much, but to do all one can is enough. I trust I can change the world. My heart is committed.

Dorothy Loretta Ann Smith
Washington, D.C. 2005

*Dorothy majored in sociology at Harvard University,
and is now a program associate at the Appleseed
Center for Law and Justice in Washington, D.C.*

Caleb Franklin

Los Angeles, California 2001

MY DAY STARTED AS IT USUALLY HAD ANY other Saturday. I woke up, ate breakfast, and watched a few minutes of television. My meal was interrupted when, over the drone of the television, I heard the loud calling of my name. I got up, following the sound into my mother's room. Little did I know that the sound was not a mere beckoning, but the herald of a monumental first experience in my life.

As I walked into her room, my mother lifted her head and informed me that our elderly neighbor needed help typing a document. Having never spent any real time with an elderly person, I was quite timid about my forthcoming fate. Nevertheless, I walked across the street and knocked on the aging wood door. As the door opened, an old and wrinkled face appeared and offered me a small twitching hand. As I shook the moldy hand, my mind convinced me I would contract some sort of bacterial infection. I proceeded into the dimly lit house, trying not to touch the old wallpaper and retro furniture.

My elderly host introduced himself as Ivor Sylvester, but insisted that I address him as Mr. Sylvester. He pointed to an old rocking chair and told me, in a mumbled and raspy voice, to take a seat. Not wanting to incite the presently docile figure into the grumpy old men I had seen so many times on television, I obliged. Sipping on prune juice and nibbling on gingersnaps in that ancient chair, I attempted to make some sort of small talk to break the silence that had taken over the room. As we talked, Mr. Sylvester told me of his many travels to exotic and wild places, of his past automobiles, and of his childhood on a farm. It seemed as if everything I was interested in reading about had already been available to me, not in a local library, but in the mind of a man that had lived across the street my whole life.

After helping with his document, I hurried home to tell my mother of my new experience. As it turns out, I started visiting Mr. Sylvester every weekend. I soon discovered that the moldy hands I had once feared were as clean, if not cleaner, than mine. The old furniture and wallpaper I once thought were from the Middle Ages were simply relics of the 1950s. The ragged door I once believed to be an ancient vestige was actually hand-built by Mr. Sylvester himself. I realized that all my fears were not based on the truth, but on the stereotypes of how elderly people were supposed to live, think, and act.

Looking back on the day I first stepped through Mr. Sylvester's door, I ascertained two certain lessons: the first, never allow stereotypes and misconceptions to bring you to fear interaction with others; the second, never neglect the knowledge, history, and wisdom elderly people possess. Now, while others may venture to museums and books for tidbits of the past, because of my experience with Mr. Sylvester I will be more than content to walk across the street to hear a piece of good old-fashioned oral history. But perhaps that day I also learned another lesson: next time, go a little lighter on the prune juice!

Caleb Franklin
Cambridge, Massachusetts 2005

Caleb majored in social studies at Harvard University.
He is currently in Bombay, India, studying on a
Gardner Fellowship.

Antonia J. Henry

Grand Rapids, Michigan 1998

THE IGNORANCE, MISUNDERSTANDING, AND prejudice of racism are steadily unraveling the fabric of America. As my generation matures, political correctness is seen as the panacea for this horrible disease. Yet, honest discourse must occur for members of different races to move towards acceptance of diversity.

Last year, I shared a room with a Caucasian girl named Elizabeth, from a small homogenous town in Indiana. We were put together out of convenience, but soon became good friends because of our common tastes in music and love of the eccentric. While studying one evening, she paused and asked me what it was like to be black. I was caught completely off guard and was unsure if I should be offended. Her honest inquiry convinced me to explain how it felt to be the only minority in a classroom when the teacher and the students attack affirmative action initiatives for integrating universities, or my thoughts when white peers say that I am an exception to the stereotype of African Americans because of my academic endeavors. Elizabeth looked down and acknowledged that, though she could never fully know what it was like, she had some empathy. Later, she related to me, in tears, the explosive reactions of her family when she dated a black classmate in middle school. For a moment we just looked at each other, not out of mutual sympathy, but with an unspoken understanding that if we were ever going to move forward in such a culturally diverse world, we and our peers would have to confront our prejudices and examine how we act towards one another.

This conversation and others like it have taught me to overcome most of my own prejudices and not assume anything about anyone. Previously, I had never thought that any of my majority peers would seriously listen to my personal experiences without discounting them as a point of view pulled out of perspective. My conversation with Elizabeth gave me hope that once people let their mental defenses relax, become willing to listen to others, and speak candidly about how their own personal experiences have been influenced by race, we can begin to overcome racism and relate to others as people, not colors.

Revoking affirmative action laws, or toughening the punishments for race-based hate crimes, or being politically correct is not going to change the way people think or bypass the prejudices that influence their behavior. If we do not make a conscious effort to accept the diversity of our fellow citizens, racism will desecrate our future. Living with Elizabeth for almost six months made me realize that we were more alike than we were different. A little conversation is a step in the right direction!

Antonia J. Henry
Boston, Massachusetts 2005

*Antonia received a bachelor's degree in microbiology
from the University of Michigan. She is scheduled
to graduate from Harvard Medical School in 2006.*

Lordserious J. Watson

Stone Mountain, Georgia 2002

I KNOW A MAN WHO WAS A FATHER AT eighteen. I know a woman who was a mother at eighteen.

I know a man who makes promises and does not keep them. I know a woman who has dedicated her life to her children.

The man left one day and told his son he would return; he didn't. The woman has taken care of her children since their birth.

The man calls his children whenever he scavenges enough money to make a long distance call. The woman tells her children that she loves them every day.

The man does not control his life. He is in and out of trouble with the law. The woman just got a promotion.

The man does not have a stable job. He has missed his son's awards and experiences. The last time he saw any of his children was about four years ago. I talked to the woman this morning.

The man is my father, the woman is my mother. Ironically, they are also my source of inspiration.

My father exhibits characteristics that I would never want to have in my life. He is irresponsible, unreliable, and an immature adult. He inspires me to do well and succeed by showing me what will happen if I don't. By calling and leaving trails of broken promises over the telephone, he forces me to realize that you cannot always expect people to do what they say they will do. I barely see him, which is comparable to the little time his father spent with him. I have noticed this trend between generations, and, because of my experiences with my father, I've decided I will not carry on the tradition.

My mother is the most dedicated person I have ever met. She teaches me that you can accomplish anything if you believe in yourself and work hard enough for it. She is determined to raise an educated family, and sacrifices her spare time to her children. She could have walked the same path as my father, but decided to take the path less taken by my family, thus motivating me to become a unique individualist. She has planted seeds of honesty and trust that flourish everyday. If at times they seem to wilt, she waters them with care and love, instilling in me a natural compassion for the well-being of others. I hope to learn more from her in the years to come, and I can only hope that, one day, my father will change his ways.

Lordserious J. Watson
Brooklyn, New York 2005

Lordserious studies engineering at Georgia Tech University. In his free time he is an aspiring hip-hop artist and has recorded several songs.

Derick Gross

Greenlawn, New York 1999

"YARD WHO?" I ASKED MY GRANDMOTHER, certain I had heard wrong. "You and I are going to the Lladro (YARD-dro) showcase store in Manhattan this Saturday," she announced one day in June two years ago. I tried as diplomatically as I could to get out of the excursion, but Grandmother is a no-nonsense lady.

When we got to the Lladro shop I realized how wrong I had been to dread the trip. The porcelain figurines for which Lladro is world-acclaimed are nothing short of exquisite. Delicate and life-like, each figurine is a miracle of craftsmanship. Grandmother stopped in front of a figurine of a brown-skinned young man in cap and gown, holding a diploma. "That's what I'm going to add to my collection when you graduate from college, sweetheart," she said, regarding me with misty eyes. "You're my first grandson who's going to do it. You're going to make me very proud one day."

I nodded, overwhelmed by her faith in me, but not convinced she was putting her money on the *right* grandson. My brother had tried community college for a while before dropping out, and of my two older male cousins, neither has gone the college route. But was I capable of doing any better? Sure, things had always come fairly easily to me – concepts and all – but I had this problem with motivation and organization. Keeping things organized, handing in assignments on time, remembering to study for exams, *wanting* to study for exams, would be a challenge. And besides, there was my circle of buddies whose opinion of me was important. Being a bookworm would simply never fly. But I wanted to validate my grandmother's vote of confidence in me, so I decided to try.

The next fall I enrolled in an Advanced Placement European history course and did well the first few weeks. In October, however, we learned that Grandmother was suffering from ovarian cancer and that the odds were very much against our having her much longer. Anger and confusion filled me, along with a sense of futility and powerlessness. What would be the point of going through all the trouble to do well if Grandmother would not be there to see it? Most of what I was doing was for her – to make her proud – wasn't it? I stopped working and my grades began to drop.

One evening a few weeks after Grandmother's surgery, I visited her. I was greeted by a frail figure with sunken eyes for whom even the trip down the stairs appeared to have been exhausting. Although her voice was weak, with enthusiasm she asked me about my history course. After all, it was the first college-level course I had attempted. I told her I was averaging a C+. "Is that your best, Derick?" she inquired. I shrugged, "Right now, yeah." She didn't judge. She knew things were hard on all of us right then, and I suddenly loved her more than I ever had.

Magically, the conflicting feelings I had about trying so hard in school and whether it was worth the effort – especially if my grandmother was going to die – seemed to dissipate. I saw my grandmother struggling with a test for which she *couldn't* prepare, a test of faith and will power. If Grandmother could do so well on a test for which she had no warning, I was darn well going to prepare for the ones I *could* prepare for.

Since then, I have taken several more AP courses and, a few weeks ago, I was designated an AP Scholar with Honors. That evening I eagerly took the AP award certificate to Grandmother. She winked with a pleased sparkle in her eye and led me upstairs to her small bedroom. Not yet out of the box, but carefully packaged in straw and cardboard, was the Lladro figurine of the boy with the diploma. "I knew it all along" she said, patting my hand tenderly.

I hope that on the day I graduate from college Grandmother has a chance to take that figurine out of its box and place it on the shelf in her living room with her few other pieces. I pray she has a chance to smile upon it for many, many years. But if she doesn't, that figurine of that boy with his diploma will still make it onto that shelf: I will place it there, with the knowledge in my heart that it got there because we *both* put it there.

Derick Gross
Huntington, New York 2005

Derick studied engineering at Columbia University.
He works at the Rainbow Chimes Early Childhood
Education and Care Center in Huntington, New York.

Ellen Tachiewaa Yiadom

Chicago, Illinois 2002

THE RED-AND-WHITE SWISSAIR PLANE prepared for landing on the cloudless August 10th afternoon at the international terminal of O'Hare Airport. A charcoal-skinned girl stared out of the window at the "New World" with round, bright, hungry eyes, ready to take the biggest bite of success her 7-and-1/2- year-old jaws could take. Her eyes remained glued to the window even after other passengers leaped from their seats with relief as the seat belt sign was turned off.

The circumstances that surrounded the arrival of this young American-to-be in the "New World" were sad, yet seemingly predestined. At the age of five she *discovered* – was never actually told – that her father had been in a car crash and had not survived. Her mother's eldest brother, the Chicagoan, and his American wife adopted her with hopes of providing her with "a better education" so that she could lead "a better life."

Coming to America from Ghana as that little girl on the plane gave me the first real sense of taking the door off the hinges when opportunity knocks. My adoptive parents gave me a new life full of opportunities. How I utilized the opportunities was my choice.

Since that first step on American soil, the choices I have made have given me access to even more opportunities. Because of my success in grade school, I received a scholarship to attend a private high school. Success in high school allowed me to participate in numerous other programs: Summer school at Choate Rosemary Hall, two summer weeks in Hamburg, Germany, for the Junge Visionen Pupil Peace Workshop, four summer weeks as a member of the LEAD Program at Wharton, two weeks with my school touring France and England, a week in Washington, D.C. as an NYLC delegate. All this success and more was the result of old-fashioned hard work and determination.

Seizing opportunities has allowed me to broaden my view of the world. By visiting other states and countries, I have been able to enjoy other cultures, yet celebrate my own. I no longer have misconceptions fed by ignorance. For example, while at Choate I realized wealthy students were not as happy and pampered as I previously imagined. After visiting Hamburg, I no longer harbored the stereotype that the German language and people were hard and difficult. I also found the French to be quite hospitable, despite previous misinformation from others.

If it is true that we are the sum of our experiences, then I must be a smorgasbord. College is my next major opportunity. I keep my parents' words in mind when I think about college: "a better education," "a better life." I hope to attend a school away from home where I will be challenged by students, like myself, who share diversified interests, a passion to learn, and a desire to grow spiritually as well as intellectually. Although the little girl on the plane is now a young woman, her passion remains as she actively searches to seize the next opportunity.

Ellen Tachiewaa Yiadom
Boston, Massachusetts 2005

*Ellen is studying government at Harvard University
and is scheduled to graduate Spring 2006. She plans to
pursue a career in entertainment law and, one day,
to run her own media company.*

Miles Alexander Johnson

Oakland, California 2004

AS A BLACK MALE IN A RIGOROUS, ACADEMIC, college preparatory high school, I have gotten used to standing out.

I no longer think twice about being the only representative of my race and culture in a given classroom or social gathering. It no longer phases me to have to field questions that assume that I can speak for all people with a skin tone similar to my own. Nor does it bother me to have to publicly challenge people's stereotypes and perceptions of my race. After so many years of bringing the African-American perspective to my high school community, and being viewed as a strong black voice within that community, I have come to embrace my status as a leader. I love guiding and supporting the younger African-American students at my school who are just now being confronted with the same responsibilities that I have come to accept and even enjoy.

Yet, as much as I cherish my culture, and as proud as I am to be a part of it, often I feel that, because of the unresolved issues surrounding racial - particularly white/black - issues within America as a whole, the color of one's skin dominates one's beliefs, accomplishments, and personality.

Traveling to Cuba provided me my first opportunity to see what it could be like to just go to school, and to know that, when I am honored and recognized, those honors celebrate purely my accomplishments - not my racial heritage.

In Cuba, they have an expression I love: "I am Cuban before anything else." The idea that one's nationality could come before any sort of racial divisions was, at first, shocking to me. As an African American, it is nearly impossible to imagine life without race as a key ingredient. So much of what I do, who I associate with, and what I value is based on my race, to the point that I might be an entirely different person if race was less of a factor in my life.

Yet, Cuba presented me with another reality: that seeing people for who they are and judging them based on their actions does not mean living in a color-blind society. In fact, there is a deep sense of cultural pride among all of the different peoples of Cuba. Both African and Spanish heritage are embraced by all. The religion of Santería is a prime example of the fusion between cultures. This religion, which is practiced, to some degree, by the majority of Cubans, both white and black, combines elements of the Yoruba traditions of Nigeria with Spanish Catholicism. There is no sharp sense of division between the white Cubans and the black Cubans as there is between black and white Americans; no matter how dissimilar they appear, their role as Cubans sets them on equal footing.

Without the divisions that race creates, the Cuban people have been able to establish a marvelous, multicultural, patchwork quilt of a community – a true melting pot. It is my hope that my college experience will enable me to make that vision a reality in this country as well.

Miles Alexander Johnson
Oakland, California 2005

Miles is studying social studies at Harvard University,
and is thinking of going to law school.

Marquise J. McGraw

Bronx, New York 2002

EARLY ONE AFTERNOON, MY MOTHER AND I decided to leave our apartment to go shopping. We got on the elevator and rode down to the first floor. When the elevator opened, to my dismay, as usual, I saw some African-American males hanging out in the lobby. These males, the community drug dealers, have established their presence in my housing project. I briefly overheard them discuss their business while I walked out the lobby, which smelled of weed as usual. My mother and I left the building and went to catch a bus.

Soon I found myself thinking about those people, and my stream of thoughts led me to the black and Hispanic youth that I work with daily as an after-school tutor. I thought about my two groups of 6th-graders – their low motivation, how they love to misbehave and refuse to follow directions. I try to figure out why my students see no inherent value in completing their homework but place much emphasis on talking to their friends, or roaming the school. I also think about my slightly more mature computer class, also full of middle school students, and I find myself smiling slightly because I am pleased with their diligence, their willingness to follow directions and complete their assignments. Then my smile disappears, and I am faced with the realization that some of my students are destined for an unfortunate future: their education is inadequate to allow them to escape the cycle of poverty and achieve higher levels of success in this society.

I often wonder where our educational system goes wrong. Is it the system itself that is failing, or is it the fact that in many of our urban African-American households the emphasis on education is at an all-time low? My 6th grade students see absolutely no connection between their homework and future success in life. Why? Is it because the school system is intentionally set up to promote failure? Possibly.

Promoting students based on age, not on their academic abilities, is part of the problem. All too often, however, in poor African-American communities such as mine, the parents are detached from their children's educational pursuits. There are many single-parent African-American families, many with mothers who grew up in poverty, and see no hope of escaping it. In this day and age, we as African Americans are faced with a multitude of opportunities that were not available to us before. However, no person can take advantage of these opportunities without an adequate education.

The value of education needs to be re-emphasized in our households. Drugs and crime will not disappear unless people start to understand that education is the way to a better life. In the near future, we must take strides to improve educational opportunities for African Americans. We also must ensure that youth see the links between hard work and success. We all must recognize that we are in control of our own destinies and that we have the power to shape our futures. In order to increase our stake in this world, we must unite and become educated. Our focus should not be so much on obtaining material things, but rather on the one thing that will endure to the end: our minds. In so doing, we will prove that we can triumph over adversity. Only then will we rise up from the clutches of poverty to the better way of life that we all deserve.

Marquise J. McGraw
Bronx, New York 2005

Marquise is studying economics at Cornell University.
He plans to earn a doctoral degree in economics
and perhaps teach.

Crystal Paul

Denver, Colorado 2004

"Will work for food...Anything Helps..."

We see these messages scribbled on cardboard signs, usually held by a grungy older man. Occasionally we drop a dime into his cup or hat, and walk briskly by him as he struggles to mumble, "God Bless." When I was younger, I wondered what these vagrants had dreamed about when they were my age. I could not fathom how they maintained the will and persistence to stand on their corners, hold up their signs, and pretend not to feel the malice in the eyes of passersby.

During my junior year in high school, I finally understood the agony of displacement. My mother quit her job and depleted the severance pay. My brother moved out, and my paycheck alone could not pay the rent. Soon we found ourselves sleeping on a couch in a warehouse pervaded by the stench and tumult of drunkenness. I could have given up; it would have been easier. Instead, I chose to persevere, to persist without fear.

Every night I comforted my mother as she cried herself to sleep. I prayed that a drunkard would not collapse on me as I slept. I would lie at my end of the couch, my feet tangled with my mother's, and let the tears fall from my eyes. Every morning, I woke up early to make sure that I would not miss the city bus if the car was not working. At school, I ignored my schoolmates who whispered and laughed about my dirty clothes or unkempt hair. Between classes I called my mother and reassured her that everything would be all right. Every moment I was not there to comfort her she seemed to lose hope; consoling her provided solace for me as well.

This was among the most significant hardships I have suffered. At times I was angry because my mother rarely put our money towards an apartment. Occasionally I was scared, terrified that I might end up like the homeless man standing on the corner. Sometimes I was miserable; hearing my mother's muffled sobs drew tears to my own eyes. But despite the anger, fear, and misery, I persisted, and I want the world to know my strength.

I ignored the ridicule from my peers. I shoved the drunkard who fell on me at night onto the floor, and I buried my head under the covers to drown out the noise. Although my troubles lingered in my mind, I managed to smile each day for my mother and for the homeless man standing behind his sign on the corner. I did not allow circumstance to defeat me, but I did allow it to teach me.

Life's hardships have taught me the wonders of kindness, fearlessness, and grace under pressure. My strength of character grows stronger with every experience, and it will never die. I will use my strength and privilege to help the weak and deprived.

Crystal Paul
New Haven, Connecticut 2005

*Crystal is majoring in comparative literature and
political science at Yale University. She is getting to see
a bit of the world and relishing life.*

Alexandra Carmel Wood

Old Bridge, New Jersey 2003

I ARRIVED FOR MY VOLUNTEER SHIFT AT St. Luke's Hospital at 10:00 am, as usual, but the sounds I heard were not those of defibrillators and nurses paging doctors. Rather, it was the loud cry of a baby resonating through the pediatrics ward.

I peered into the quaint, star-filled hospital room and was taken aback by the sight of a small person wearing a thin, blue and white polka-dot hospital gown, standing in the steel crib. Tears rushed down her mahogany face while her braided hair lay calmly on her perfectly shaped head. Her bright brown eyes were the size of saucers, filled with such passion and drive. Yet they showed the pains of her Leukemia-stricken body.

Never before having had contact with such an ill child, I approached her with caution and noticed that she was actually studying me. She pondered her next move, and decided to give me the nod of approval by turning her rage-filled eyes into small windows onto her distressed soul. Slowly, I felt a connection, and her cries became a language that only the heart could understand. I went to the crib and fumbled with the child-safety locks until the gate of the crib opened. Carefully embracing her, I lifted her small body out of the crib. An instant bond was made, and I felt as if I had known her forever.

After a few moments, her cries faded away, and the only sound left was the soft murmur of her breathing. I carefully placed her back into the crib and proceeded down the rainbow-colored corridor to the play therapy room, where I usually worked. Suddenly, I heard the harsh sound of her sobs coming from the hospital room. I saw the nurses run to her, but she continued to let out her loudest cries. After gathering as many toys from the playroom as I possibly could, I rushed back into her room, goodies in hand, and saw her eyes light up like lamps turned on by a switch.

I took her out of her bed and held her in my arms. As she played with the toys I had given her, I noticed that her tears of sadness had turned into tears of joy. Slowly, she drifted into a sound slumber, and I placed her back into her crib.

As I sat in the room and watched her sleep, I realized that all she really needed was a person to spend time with and someone to show her affection. Her cries had compelled me to act, and in doing so I understood that I could put my hesitations aside in order to help others. This made me realize that volunteering is the activity that has the most significance for me.

Later that day, I looked at my watch and noticed that it was one o'clock. I had spent the entire morning with a person I had never met before, and one who could not communicate by words. As I left pediatrics, the sounds I heard were not those of defibrillators and nurses paging doctors; rather, it was the giggle of a baby echoing through the ward.

Alexandra Carmel Wood
Cambridge, Massachusetts 2005

*Alexandra studies government at Harvard University.
In her spare time she volunteers with the Cambridge
Student Partnerships, helping find employment
and social services for those in need in the Boston area.*

Robert J. Smith III

Plantation, Florida 2005

THEY DON'T LIKE IT WHEN I TALK — OR WHEN
anyone does, for that matter. Talking always seems
to get you in trouble. There used to be more
talking once, talk of peace and love and justice.
Jesus talked. King talked. Mandela talked.
See where it got them.

For the longest time I was too scared to talk.
That was when I couldn't hear my own voice.
I had never used it. I stayed quiet for fear of what
they might do to me. Then I realized, now is
not the time for silence. We need to talk – now
more than ever.

It's my turn. Listen.

I am a man whose citizenship does not trump
his conscience, who will not fill up his gas
tank with the blood of Iraqi women and children,
who wonders why he should be proud to be
an American when America isn't proud of him,
whose black skin will never be traded in for
advancement or prestige, who isn't sure if he
believes in God or if He/She/non-gendered deity
believes in him, who worries if he'll ever be
black enough or queer enough or just enough for
anyone, who grew up without a father and never
needed one (my mother made me a man!),
who loves men while my church calls it a sin, who
is ashamed his government has sold its integrity
to the highest bidder, who thinks Bentonville,
Arkansas is the greatest threat to America, who
fears one-party rule and two-party politics,
who cried when he read *Go Tell it on the Mountain*,
who thinks nice guys should finish first for a
change, who thinks the, like, pervasiveness of the
word "like" has, like, no redeeming social value,
who is sure Satan, Leibniz, and Newton conspired
to invent calculus to wreck his GPA, who thinks
Al Sharpton isn't as crazy as the pundits think,
who doesn't understand why "sodomy" became a
word but "Gomorrah-y" hasn't, who is angry
the election came down to men kissing, who stood
in line for five hours to cast a vote for the man
who would lose, who thinks Ronald Reagan's
silence on AIDS was the worst kind of treason,
who thinks OJ did it, who dances to Nirvana
and Outkast and reggaeton, who loves Baldwin
and DuBois and Marquez, who is every white
guy's "black friend," who is dying to know
how Kelis's milkshake brings all the boys to the
yard, who thinks Jon Stewart is the funniest
man alive and that Leno is overrated, who cannot
understand why the South votes against its
economic interest every four years, who is not a
fag but a man, who is not macho but still a man,
who will have a limp wrist and a strong mind,
who wonders how many Black Democratic
Socialist Southern Baptist agnostic queers do you
know, who will not rest until the bombs do,
who will raise hell until he gets what he wants –
what everyone wants: everything.

I wish I had more time to talk: 500 words are
never enough.

Robert J. Smith III
Fort Lauderdale, Florida 2005

Robert is studying Africana studies and urban studies at Brown University. He plans to study sociology at the graduate level and perhaps enter academia.

Autumn Joy Anderson

Rapid City, South Dakota 2003

AS A SINGLE MOM RAISING THREE BIRACIAL children in Laramie, Wyoming – where diversity is unheard of – while attending and paying for law school and providing for us kids, she amazed me. She was my mother and father, teacher and best friend, and, most of all, my role model. Alone, she organized women's rights groups and low-income housing occupants, constantly lobbying for their rights. Her strength inspired and empowered me to become a reflection of her.

So when my mother suffered from a manic episode, my image of her crashed as surely as the world around her. Her mental imbalance transformed her from the person I saw looking back at me in the mirror to a virtually unrecognizable shadow. Her mind became unsure and childlike, the exact opposite of her intimidating intelligence and natural confidence. Her emaciated body lost all familiarity and previous health. She rambled about suicide, believed the television was interacting with her, and, most disturbingly, treated me as if I were her mother. One day, after rear-ending a car, she continued to drive like it had never happened. Baffled, I brought the accident to her attention. Blatantly ignoring the huge dent and broken taillight, she simply said, "I didn't hit that car, God wouldn't have let me."

Soon, I could no longer hear the comforting euphemisms that denial had been singing in my ear, for interrupting the melody was the realization that my mother had lost all sense of reality. I could only hear the ringing of the breaking glass, which I used to emulate my mother. Everything continued to get progressively worse; the police were regulars at our door, and my mom's firm hadn't seen her for months.

My mother had been the one keeping our family's continuity, but when she got sick my siblings and I were forced to move in with our estranged father. The guilt and hate that I felt were inseparably intertwined and directed toward her. The spiral of hateful, hurtful, and frightened emotions twirled in my solar plexus and spewed out of my mouth like venom, bitter and vengeful toward the only person I had actively loved: my mother.

I began to passively love and actively hate everyone around me, shutting off from all people, viewing them as fake, fickle, and phony, immersing myself in anything that couldn't hurt me, or worse, couldn't be taken from me. I had built my life upon my mother's strength, not my own, and when her bipolar disorder took over her life, it left me with nothing but myself.

Slowly, stepping away from the reflection of my mother's strength and pulling the broken pieces of mirror out of my feet motivated me to find myself. I began to excel in school for me rather than for my mother's affirming smile and uplifting praise. Not being able to lean on her made me become independent, strong, and confident in triumphs and failures. To say it simply, I grew up.

My experience with my mother taught me to be the kind of person who will celebrate with someone on their happiest day, cry with them on their saddest, and counsel them when it may be their last. This taught me about the quality and content of my character, and the strength of my ability to love. What defines me is not my heritage, grades, or extra-curricular activities. Rather, it is how I rise to every obstacle – be it a tournament or a test. Now I know that I am capable of rising to the occasion.

My mother and I are now rebuilding our relationship – despite thousands of miles and hurtful memories between us. Regardless of her retired law degree, her medications and her mood swings, she remains a powerful and inspirational woman. With everything stripped away, what remains is the true her, a beautiful human being – a human being I myself am striving to be.

Autumn Joy Anderson
Berkeley, California 2005

Autumn is studying African-American studies, rhetoric and sociology at the University of California, Berkeley.

J. Paulson Tuffet

Miami, Florida 1997

THE DECLINE OF AMERICAN PUBLIC education is a ghost that continues to haunt America. For generations, Americans perceived the link between universal public education and social mobility and success. That link needs to be restored by efforts that revitalize the public school system. With a wholesale redesign of the very infrastructure of the school system as the ultimate goal, America must begin its reform in the inner city schools.

For too long, the implicit general consensus has been that the larger American community has no responsibility for addressing such black or minority problems as poor educational attainment and subsequent poverty. In general, America has disregarded that those problems are the result of centuries of cultural deformation and economic deprivation under racist laws. The plight of racial and ethnic minorities is attributable to more generalized failures in society, primarily in the field of basic education. The search for efforts to improve the condition of minorities must then focus in this general and difficult area, and the answers can come only gradually as basic institutions, attitudes, customs, and practices are changed. Acquired disabilities, by which minorities enter American society already at a disadvantage, must be destroyed.

Acquired disabilities – the very real culture of poverty that equips many children of the ghetto and barrio with attitudes making them unfit for the mainstream community – are the most difficult, because the most subtle, of all obstacles. Nothing less than a program to liberate denizens of the ghettos and barrios from those environments, family by family, is likely to succeed. And any such program must be rooted in the most fundamental institution in America: the school.

The American contract of equality of opportunity and egalitarianism has been breached. Inner city students, who are disproportionately minorities, are being cheated out of the great equalizer in American society and the lubricant of the wheels of social mobility: education. The transgression includes a lack of financial resources, but emanates from the essential methodology of inner city schools. Often inner city schools employ dislocated, unrelated, intimidated teachers who do not want to put forth the time and effort mandatory to tap into the intellectual consciousness of inner city youth. The result is disgruntled, discouraged, and disillusioned teachers who have resigned themselves to the perception that the children in their classes are hopelessly inept.

This translates into the skewed message that is being relayed to inner city youth – that it is not only acceptable but, indeed, inherent that they fail. When students cannot reach reasonable standards, they are lowered. Why? It is simple for both the student and the teacher to accept and excuse poor performance. The real challenge, and, consequently, the real success, is derived from addressing underachievement with consistently high standards and comprehensive educational support. Otherwise, schools are failing to prepare students for the harsh reality of the indiscriminate, inconsiderate, incessant struggle of life. And failure to prepare is preparation for failure.

The effect of redeeming inner city education would be positive and far reaching. Inner city youth would begin to be empowered with the tools necessary not only to survive but to excel in mainstream society. The defeat of many other societal ills, such as economic class stratification and family decay, would follow. This time in America would signal the dissemination of a new message to the downtrodden and disadvantaged: hope and aspiration rather than resignation and apathy.

J. Paulson Tuffet
Washington, D.C. 2005

Paulson earned his bachelor's degree in economics from the University of Pennsylvania, with a minor in African-American studies. He is currently studying at Georgetown University Law Center.

Samuel Zenebe Alemayehu

Beltsville, Maryland 2004

I AM SAMUEL HAILE-GEBRAIL ZENEBE Alemayehu, also known as "Chicken Sam," the mighty trainer of fighting roosters in Addis Ababa, Ethiopia, where I was born. There, I was master of King Theodrows, the champion rooster. There, my parents struggled to provide my four siblings and me the best they could offer.

Life was hard in Ethiopia. Many of my friends "owned" their own houses, portable plastic boxes on the street comers of Addis. Although my mother said my friends were "homeless," I cared little about their status, and trained my roosters and shared my shoeshine stand with them. From six to noon I went to school; after school, I shined shoes with my friends and worked with the roosters. When the sun set, my friends went to the soccer field, but while they played, I was the rooster master, always finding ways to communicate with these magnificent creatures. If I won at the competitions, I could either claim the losing rooster, or earn money that would pay for my school materials. Most of the time, I won.

In the morning, the roosters crowed, "Ku, Ku, Kulu." They were my alarm clock at 6 am every day. As I worked with them, I learned to channel my strength and focus my mind on my task. Then, when I was 10, something changed. My favorite, King Theodrows, lost a cockfight – and his life. Suddenly, my rooster's pain seemed unbearable to me; I began to question whether I wanted to continue cockfighting as a form of income or sport.

At about the same time, one day a stranger posed a mathematical riddle to me while I worked on his shoes. For days, as I struggled with the riddle, I understood that I could use my mind as a competitive tool, much as I had used the roosters. I realized that I had outgrown the cockfighting, and, instead, made the roosters my pets. I trained them in the art of running rather than fighting, and soon thereafter I began to redirect my energy to other goals.

One day five years ago, my father announced that he would be leaving Ethiopia. He would come to the United States and have the rest of us join him two years later. In America, I would learn to train another "rooster" who would be as brave as King Theodrows, but who would rise above the competition – my mind.

I am amazed at the opportunities that my new schools in America provide. Yet, I am saddened that people in my community are branded incapable of success because of their race or background. I work hard, always inspired by those who passed before me, and hoping to inspire those who come after me. Here, there is nothing I take for granted. Everything is a privilege. I will help better my community in America and also, eventually, I will go back home to help the friends I left behind. For now, as I reach out to touch the stars, part of me will always remember that I am "Chicken Sam."

Samuel Zenebe Alemayehu
Stanford, California 2005

Sam studies mechanical engineering and economics at Stanford University. He still maintains a connection with birds, and he looks forward to having another pet rooster sometime soon.

Victor A. Davis

Washington, D.C. 2001

MY GREATEST FEAR IS GROWING UP AND being a terrible father.

My father walked out on my mother many years ago, and my mother, my sister, and I have undertaken the task of building and nurturing our family. I used to hate my father because I was different. In elementary school I was the only child in my class whose parents were separated. The pain subsided in junior high school, and today I bear no evil against my father. Today, that which made me different as a child is that which most I cherish.

I am different. Not many other young adults can say that they appreciate their family, but I do. My mother, in order to provide for my sister and me, works two jobs, and although I wish she didn't, I now welcome the responsibility and the opportunity this has given me.

While I will not say that I have been a father to my sister, in my mother's absence I have had to assume parent-like responsibilities in order to ensure the stability of our home. My mother never forced me to assume such responsibilities; she is too considerate, and she believes that we should grow up having had a "normal childhood." She would never ask for our help, but it was needed. So, when I was 16 I decided to get a part-time job after school working at a community activism organization. With the money I earned, I helped to buy groceries, pay for my and my sister's weekly supply of lunch, and I managed to save about $20 a week for miscellaneous items.

My mother is truly the matriarch of my family, and initially I took her absence to mean freedom. I would do as I pleased, and allow my sister to do the same. However, as time passed I realized this is not the way my mother would have her house. So, at night, when she worked, I did my part to restore order. I had to be an enforcer, and for someone like me who loves to make jokes, it was hard. Initially, I found it awkward to tell my sister to get off the phone and start her homework. It was challenging to help her complete her homework while mine was yet to be done.

Every night, after coming home from school or work, I had to prepare dinner and complete whatever tasks my mother needed. Sometimes that meant going to an information session at my sister's school, or picking her up from a late rehearsal. Although challenging, in retrospect I have welcomed each moment.

On weekends, when all three of us are together, there is an overwhelming sense of family. We all deeply appreciate each other's company because we all have a very thorough understanding of family. Family are the people who give of themselves to help others. I wonder sometimes if I will be able to make the sacrifices my mother does. She is the most selfless person I know, and I wish, one day, to be a tenth of the person she is.

I once hated my father. Today our relationship has improved, but I can't help but pity him: he had all the riches in the world – a great family – and he missed out.

Victor A. Davis
Princeton, New Jersey 2005

Victor studied economics at Princeton University, and is now employed as a business analyst in the New York office of Accenture, a global management consulting and outsourcing firm.

Veronica H. Threadgill

Brooklyn, New York 2001

BECAUSE I GREW UP IN NEW YORK, ONE might assume that I've seen diversity in every aspect of life. I wish that were true.

The sad fact is that, in a city so diverse and so full of culture, far too many children lead insular lives. I grew up in a completely homogenous neighborhood; everyone I came across for the first eleven years of my life was just like me. I didn't realize how broad this problem was until I started working at a YMHA as a camp counselor and a mentor in the after-school program. Most of the children I met there were from very similar backgrounds. All of their friends were the same race and religion; their schools lacked any mix of cultures and communities. This is a problem because intolerance, hate, and prejudice spring from ignorance. If a person comes from childhood having no first-hand experience with people who are different, they aren't likely to be unbiased adults.

This brings me to my project – a combination of after-school program and summer camp to help bring together kids from all kinds of backgrounds.

There have always been programs catering specifically to upper-middle-class kids, and programs for underprivileged kids. The problem with both is that they still tend to separate children by race, neighborhood, and socioeconomic background. My vision is a program that brings together children from all different parts of a city, and gives them a chance to know each other. It would incorporate different programs for different age groups, including story time, show-and-tell, art projects, trips to parks and museums.

A big part of the program would be discussions about the cultures of the kids involved. These wouldn't be classes taught by an instructor whose job is to teach kids about other communities; it would be a discussion among the children, to talk about what makes them special. Each day or week would have a different theme, such as holidays or favorite foods. Guests, such as parade and festival coordinators, chefs from various ethnic restaurants, and exchange students, could come to share their stories and talk about what they do. This would be a way for the kids to spend time with other children and learn from them. It would also be a chance for them to experience the lives and backgrounds of other people in a setting that would help them realize that, no matter how different we seem, we're all the same. This is a knowledge most of us start out with, but lose as we grow up in very uniform environments.

There's no reason for any child to grow up ignorant of the customs, holidays, and values of people from different backgrounds. Rather, children should be exposed to them so they can come to accept others and be prepared to enter the new globalized world.

Veronica H. Threadgill
Brooklyn, New York 2005

Veronica received degrees in accounting and financial services from Roger Williams University. She is currently working for KPMG, one of the Big Four accounting firms, as an auditor. She loves working with children, and hopes to someday run a foundation dedicated to helping kids in her favorite city – New York.

Brandon L. Cook

Budapest, Hungary 2003

I CAN VIVIDLY REMEMBER WITNESSING THE manifestation of human depravity and hearing the first words my mother said to me: "Pack your bags. We'll be leaving soon." Within a week, my mother, brother and I were on a plane, leaving my father and home in Islamabad, Pakistan. As with countless others, the events of September 11 irrevocably changed my life, but for me in a more direct way.

Over the next five months, my family and I endured searching for a home in the States, coping with a new school, and constantly worrying about whether we would see my father and home ever again. Eventually, we pulled through and were able to return to Islamabad. In rejoining my old life, there was the joy of seeing my father and of returning to my school and friends, but also an ever-present uncertainty and disconnection. It's true, you can never go home again.

Then, on a Saturday morning, March 17, my life changed again. That morning, a bombing at the International Protestant Church resulted in five deaths. Within the hour, we learned that a fellow classmate and her mother were two of the victims of this act of terrorism. This was the family that welcomed us on the first day of our arrival in Islamabad, over a year ago, and that sat next to us on the flight home. It is hard to believe that their young girl, who had such a bright future ahead of her, and her mother, who only returned to make her children happy, were both gone.

Pushing beyond our broken spirits, my family took in the youngest of this shattered family while his father recovered. As he lay in my room, I, only ten feet away, tried to comprehend what he was going through. Losing a mother and sister in a single day, and so violently, was something I could barely handle.

A few days later the message came down that we would be leaving Islamabad again, but this time permanently. Because of the role my family had taken, we were allowed to accompany this family to the States, where their lost members could have an appropriate funeral.

Over the past few days my mind had been wiped clean. Now, the only thing left rattling inside me is the hum of the freight plane and the memory of the people who were snatched from us just three days ago.

On the plane, strapped into my harness, I glanced over to the sleeping father and son, who had just lost a wife, daughter, mother and sister, and to the mother and daughter, resting eternally, in two white boxes only fifty feet away. Tear-filled, I came to the painful realization that life is a merciless and unyielding, yet magnificent, force. Through it, we come to terms with the fact that we must be strong and cannot let the sorrows keep us from living. We must take in all that comes to us, not dwelling in it, but growing from it, bettering each other and ourselves.

Brandon L. Cook
New Haven, Connecticut 2005

*Brandon is studying linguistics at Yale University.
He plans to get a Ph.D. in linguistics, or perhaps go
to law school. Brandon spent most of his youth in
Islamabad, Pakistan, but his family is now stationed
in Frankfurt, Germany.*

Misha M. Mutizwa

Rocky River, Ohio 2001

A STANDARD DICTIONARY WOULD DEFINE the word inequality as "disparity of distribution or opportunity." An individual's recognition of specific inequalities depends largely on that person's standpoint in life. My perspective on contemporary American society is one that has allowed me to notice two considerably significant inequalities – those based upon race and economic class.

As recently as middle school, I can remember asking my older sister, "What's the big deal about race?" Up to that point, I had always questioned the existence of racial discrimination. Perhaps I had been too young to notice how frequently my father was followed by a police officer while driving, or how often people stared disapprovingly at my white mother while I was sitting in her shopping cart at the grocery store. More likely, however, is that I was simply being naive. Since then, I have forced myself to deal with the racial inequality in American society.

My life has enabled me to be in close contact with people from varying economic backgrounds. What I have seen has shown me that, in America, money means everything. To me, the idea of someone paying close to $40,000 a year to attend a private university is obscene. Yet, the majority of students at many of the nation's top colleges find that their parents are earning too much money to qualify for *any* sort of aid. In this country, there are also thousands of high school seniors who spend every free moment working at part-time jobs in an effort to handle rising college costs. The present economic climate in America is one in which economic disparity runs rampant.

My perspective on contemporary American society has allowed me to recognize the deep-seated injustice found in all types of inequality. A purpose central to America's existence has been an individual's right to pursue happiness and freedom. Today, however, some people are basically handed these rights before others have even had the opportunity to reach for them.

In college, I plan to major in public policy while focusing on the administration of justice. Public policy is a major that provides students with the skills necessary to promote change in society. Although I'm not exactly sure what I will do with my life following college, I know that I hope to make as much of a difference as I can in any area of inequality. I am fully aware that some type of inequality will always exist. One of my goals, however, is to minimize its existence.

Misha M. Mutizwa
Durham, North Carolina 2005

*Misha studied public policy, with a concentration in
health policy, at Duke University. He is currently
enrolled in a dual degree MD/MPH program at Duke
University School of Medicine. He plans to pursue
a career in health policy.*

Jamar Campbell

Aurora, Colorado 2000

IT WAS HORRIBLY UNBELIEVABLE.

Even though my family had faced many financial difficulties in the past, nothing I had faced before could even remotely compare to this: I was living in a homeless shelter. My parents' tremendous credit difficulties, constant money problems, and the unreasonably high price of rent in the city landed us in a homeless shelter. Incredibly, throughout this entire ordeal I was able to attend a prestigious private school with some of the wealthiest kids in Colorado.

My 5-month stay in the homeless shelter left an indelible impression on me that altered my perspective and goals. I made many vows to achieve a better life for myself and my family, and to use my mind to rise out of the abject poverty I faced. The situation and the pressure involved forced me to be introspective and re-examine my goals in life.

Ironically, I experienced this revelation as I mopped the floor of the shelter in the dead of the night – one of the few times I had to reflect.

I had just gotten home from a basketball game. I had ridden the Dawson school bus to a busy intersection to await the city bus and ride it to the shelter. Like every other day, within a matter of hours I went from a world of gross extravagance to one of abject poverty, filled with people struggling to survive. Every day I trekked this journey, and none of my schoolmates suspected that I lived in these conditions. None were aware that I processed untold insights when we had class discussions on homelessness and similar matters. Naturally, I thought it was insane that I should be attending this school given the situation I was in, but my parents insisted that I continue to attend. We did have a significantly reduced tuition based on our income, but still, considering our dire financial status it didn't seem feasible to travel 30 miles everyday, from one bus to another. Nevertheless, I continued this routine, and in hindsight I am glad I stayed at the school because, despite the many seemingly insurmountable obstacles, it gave me motivation and opportunity.

That night at the shelter I had to wait for the people to clear the cafeteria. Every family was assigned a chore, and my brothers had once again failed to mop. My dad was working late, so I had to assume the responsibility of mopping the floor at midnight on a school night, finally going to bed at 1:30 am.

As I mopped, I remember feeling overwhelmed, angry, and sorry for myself. Once again, there I was engaged in the same strenuous and monotonous labor that I had completely grown sick of. I wanted to cry, yet I knew I had to be strong and could not afford to be vulnerable. Soon the realization that my feelings of bitterness were useless helped replace my dismal hopelessness with a determination to do what I knew I had to do in order to survive.

Since then, my parents started working more hours, they both got jobs, and things have been a whole lot better. Although seven of us still live in a one-room apartment, I am grateful that I have at least a place to stay and I am able to further my studies. It is amazing how a totally impulsive person like me was transformed into an introspective and pensive person. After that experience, while remaining grounded by the past harsh realities, I became even more passionate and idealistic. And throughout, I was humbled and blessed with a newfound recognition of what I had to achieve for myself.

Jamar Campbell
Chicago, Illinois 2005

Jamar graduated from Northwestern University with a degree in economics and political science. Now, when he is not teaching test preparation at Niles West High School in Chicago, he is a vigorous aspiring essayist and opinion columnist.

Morgan G. Harper

Columbus, Ohio 2001

FOR AS LONG AS I CAN REMEMBER, THE question "What are you?" has been a part of my life. People I just met ask me this before they even know my name or where I'm from. This inquiry makes me feel alienated because it is a constant reminder that, for many people, my defining characteristic is my skin color. Recently, however, I have been able to answer this question with an enlightened sense of confidence. *What Are You?* is a chronicle of the experiences of several multiracial young people, and it influenced my outlook by letting me know that I am not alone in my struggle to find an identity.

The search for common ties with others can be extremely difficult for anyone, but especially for those who are multiracial. I know firsthand how hard this pursuit can be. Being African-American and Caucasian, I defy categorization. I cannot define who I am by checking one single box on an application. I have never walked into a room and found someone who looked like me. As a citizen of the United States, where everything is defined in terms of black and white, I don't have the luxury of choosing a side on the color line that still divides our country. Instead, I have to balance myself carefully along this line. If I journey too far to one side, I am reproached In black social settings, my caramel-colored skin is just light enough and my brown hair just straight enough that I immediately stand out. In white settings, the distinction between me and others is more subtle, but equally hurtful. As much as we, as a society, have progressed in our acceptance of minorities, the fact remains that a great majority of our social groups are based on race. Between people of the same race there is a sense of community one cannot find anywhere else; for *me* that has been a void I have never been able to fill.

What Are You? filled that void. This book offered me the sense of community that has always eluded me. I became lost in its pages and its stories of people like me. I was excited to learn of a girl who was African-American, German, and French, and who was just as unsure of herself as I am when it comes to knowing who to date.

I felt a bond with others who, like me, are tired of being seen as nothing more than an exotic commodity. I read voraciously about teenagers who have had to deal with the same questioning stares when walking with parents whose skin colors are different from their own. I was struck to know that other young people, too, have felt like outsiders at their own extended-family functions.

Within these stories I found myself, I found my identity, and I found the confidence to be honest with myself about a question that has followed me for as long as I can remember.

So what am I? I'm Morgan Gray Harper. I'm known as "Morgan" to most of the world, "Morgs" to some of my friends, and "Mo" to my family. I have a horrible fear of heights. I am ruthlessly sarcastic. I am more sensitive than most people think. I'm an overachiever who's lazy when it comes to housework. I have an unhealthy obsession with the Spanish language. I'm too impatient, and I'm about to embark on one of the biggest transitions in my life, and I'm a little scared. I am neither black nor white, and I will not solely classify myself as either race.

I am multiracial, and I refuse to deny any part of who I am.

Morgan G. Harper
Cambridge, Massachusetts 2005

*Morgan studied community health and Spanish at
Tufts University. She now works as a paralegal
for the Federal Trade Commission in Washington,
D.C. She intends to pursue a graduate degree in public
policy and eventually to attend law school as well.*

Ilisten M. Jones

Carson, California 2000

GROWING UP AS ONE OF SIX CHILDREN WITH a single parent living on a fixed income has never been easy. Yet, that is the living situation that formed the context of my upbringing and helped to mold my mentality.

I was reared in a low-income neighborhood just outside of Los Angeles, where role models in professional fields were scarce. Many of the young people in my neighborhood were content to find minimum wage jobs right after high school – that is, if they planned on completing high school.

Numerous stigmas and stereotypes were attached to my community and the people living there, which made it a daily struggle for me to overcome my predicament. I woke up at 5:30 every morning so that I could catch the bus to attend school outside my area, and on the way home I devised clever ways to avoid the numerous "distractions." Some days, just concentrating on my homework was a hurdle because of the daily rhythmic gunshots. Other days, I had to force myself to get out of bed and enter the air of hopelessness that engulfed my community.

Yet, I refused to let my socioeconomic circumstances dictate my future or be excuses for failure.

My staunch refusal to settle for anything less than my personal best stems directly from my mother, a Jamaican immigrant. As head of the household, my mother always made sure that her children were provided for, which was not always easy considering the dearth of resources she had to work with. She sacrificed a lot to ensure that her children were in a position to receive a better education than she was able to receive, and she never allowed me to let our financial instability stand in the way of pursuing my goals. Although she could never teach by example since she never graduated from college, she managed to instill in each of her children a desire to seek higher education. And that desire made me a unique specimen, something of an oddity in my community, as if having the name Ilisten – pronounced "I-Listen," and intended by my mother to be taken literally – weren't enough.

Many of my classmates shunned me for having such "big dreams," as they called them, and they ridiculed me for trying to defy the odds that society had stacked against me. They failed to realize that I was only trying to end the vicious cycle that low-income communities often induce. Their doubts and discouraging comments caused me to reconsider my plans many times, but each time I decided that I had come too far to let anyone dissuade me.

As I began formulating my plans to study medicine, I developed an affinity for studying plastic surgery, which intrigued me. To get some hands-on experience, I spent five weeks as a member of the Stanford Youth Environmental Science Program (SYESP). I was drawn to the many opportunities it offered – the chance to hear lectures by Stanford professors, to study under the auspices of a Rhodes Scholar physician, and to participate in labs involving human cadavers.

The program's directors stressed the importance of behaving altruistically and of using one's abilities to assist others. Armed with this insight, I began investigating ways that would enable me, as a future physician, to assist my community while obtaining esteem in the medical community. My prolonged search led me to the Shriner's Hospital in Los Angeles.

I first went to the hospital with fellow members of my school's Key Club to help the young patients make arts and crafts for Halloween. Little did I know that helping them carve pumpkins and make trick-or-treat bags would lead to the end to my frustrating search. Some of the patients at the hospital were low-income burn victims whose families were plagued by tremendous medical bills. Others faced language barriers. But the smiles and hugs I received from them conveyed their gratitude and led to one of the most significant epiphanies of my life, solidifying my interest in medicine and sparking my interest in performing charity community outreach work as a reconstructive surgeon.

I have since forsaken my plans to perform plastic surgery solely for my patients' cosmetic whims; instead, I hope to use reconstructive surgery to better the lives of victims of severe burns, tragic accidents, and wars. I realize that many people, including many young children, are in dire need of such services. Being able to give back to my community would bring things full circle because I have personally witnessed many people suffer from treatable conditions simply because of their inability to afford medical insurance. Working for an organization such as Interplast, a non-profit medical organization that provides reconstructive surgery free of charge in developing countries, would enable me to help even more people.

I will be successful when I rise above my socioeconomic status while still remaining close to my community so that my experience may help others overcome the difficulties I once knew.

Ilisten M. Jones
Carson, California 2005

Ilisten graduated from Harvard University with a degree in biochemical sciences. After working a year as a research associate at the Center for Healthier Children, Families and Communities at the University of California, Los Angeles, she is now attending Harvard Medical School.

Errol C. Saunders II

Los Angeles, California 2002

THE 21ST CENTURY HOLDS MUCH MORE promise for African Americans than any other century in American history. Finally, the status quo supports the eradication of racism in all forms, de jure segregation has been universally abolished, and more of us than ever are in the position to help ourselves rather than being a drain on the state. But one menace still stands in the way of full-fledged African-American participation in the American dream – our selves.

True, the United States is a nation of immigrants, many of whom have succeeded in their surrogate world. However, the unique circumstances surrounding the arrival of the black man on American shores have set him apart from the mass of immigrants. While many of them were faced with extreme conditions at home and fled to America with the hope of a better life, quite the opposite is true for the African American. He alone was transported against his will to this nation, and for 250 years he toiled here without hope, without betterment, and without even those benefits normally afforded to beings solely by nature of their humanity. Such a dismal past has inevitably stunted our growth as a community, and continues to do so.

Today, even after all the barriers of slavery have been removed, we maintain a certain slave mentality – the mentality that the world is against us. It is not one of servitude or inferiority, but rather one that produces, in effect, both of the aforementioned mindsets. Perhaps in 1865, or even in 1965, such a mindset was necessary to promote the winds of change, but now, in post-Civil Rights America, it has become more of hindrance than a unifying force.

For the black man in 2002, it is more important to realize that our participation in the American dream, denied our ancestors for so many years, is indeed possible, perhaps even probable, should we choose to participate. Yes, remnants of the old way may still exist, in our minds, in our nation, and maybe even in the rest of the world, but we cannot limit ourselves any longer by our preoccupation with the past. The past is done, it cannot be fixed, and the world's feeling of guilt will not continue forever while we try to get our act together. We must focus on the bright future that lies ahead of us.

For our race, daresay our people, to succeed in the "white man's world" we must believe that we are capable of doing so. Belief in one's self is the paramount pillar of the American idealism of the 21st Century; luckily, it comes with no color lines or wealth requirements attached.

THE COLONY AGENT
IN LONDON WHO
INTERESTED
GOVERNOR YALE
IN THE COLLEGE AND
COLLECTED LARGE
GIFTS FOR THE LIBRARY

Errol C. Saunders II
New Haven, Connecticut 2005

Errol studies political science at Yale University.
He hopes to be a teacher of history and civics, or maybe
a professor of urban planning.

Angela A. Smedley

Ann Arbor, Michigan 2000

THE RACE OF PEOPLE THAT I ASSOCIATE with has been an influential factor in my life for as long as I can remember.

Growing up as a "mixed" child – my dad is black and my mom is white – has had its subtle and not-so-subtle effects on my behavior. Throughout most of my life, I think that I have related more to the white part of my racial heritage, and it hasn't been until recently that I have connected with the black side.

I was shy as a child, and I knew very little about my ethnicity, which made me hesitant to talk about racial issues. The majority of people in my life were white, and, unfortunately, the black people I did know seemed either to be quite rowdy, or mean, or troublemakers, so I did not get too involved with them. These people included students at my elementary school, some of my dad's friends, and my aunts, whom my dad didn't get along with too well. This resulted in me not being comfortable with, and certainly not being proud of, my color. I remember when one of my good friends in second grade asked if I was black or just really, really tan, and I answered "tan," hoping she would believe it. Even now I am sometimes shy or self-conscious when I meet new people, and I am still discovering how many ways race affects my thoughts and actions.

When my parents divorced when I was in seventh grade, my confusion and uncertainty grew worse. I was then living solely with my mom, and though I "grew up white," I have never really felt comfortable in a large group of white people because my skin is clearly a different color. However, the same thing is true for me in a group of black people: while I am more comfortable because I do not stand out for my skin tone, I often do stand out because of the way I talk and the way I have been brought up. So, although I like being with both groups for different reasons, and I enjoy being able to experience both worlds, sometimes the experiences are not pleasant.

There have been several instances when people have commented on my skin color, some in a rude way, some in a complimentary way. Once, I was at a basketball game when a guy from another school came up to me and said "What are you, mixed or something?" I was taken aback by his boldness and simply said yes. His question made me self-conscious; it made me wonder what it is that we first see when we meet somebody. In people's minds am I considered black? Or do they think of me as mixed? Additionally, certain expectations seem to come with your color. If you're black, this includes being a good athlete and a good dancer. For example, at one of our school dances a girl said, "I hate dancing next to black people; they always make you look bad." It was a funny comment, but it made me feel awkward because I'm not necessarily one of the most skilled dancers at our school.

Since my sophomore year, I have grown more comfortable talking about my race and more at ease with my color. In fact, race is something that really intrigues me; I love hearing about how race has affected other people's lives, since it has had so great an impact on my own. My race is something that is very important to me, perhaps because I struggled with it for so long. Being mixed is not just a descriptive racial term. It is who I am.

Angela A. Smedley
New York, New York 2005

Angela studied sociology and African-American studies at Harvard University. Now she is a legal assistant at Willkie, Farr & Gallagher in Manhattan.

Maria I. Velazquez

Springfield, Massachusetts 2000

OVER THE SUMMER I WAS STRIPPED AWAY like an onion – a gradual pruning of all but the essentials. I was purified.

Now, I'm finding out, it is hard to come home again.

I spent the summer as far away from home as I could get: two weeks in New Mexico as a Student Challenge Award Recipient, contemplating unknown constellations, and four weeks as a scholarship student at Xavier University in New Orleans.

Leaving home was the scariest part. I have made myself malleable; I am the good student, the understanding friend, the dutiful daughter. I have always defined myself in terms of others: the ways they understood me was the way I was. It is so easy to do that. It is an easing of the mind, a process of surrender, a fading into oblivion, a surrender that kept me from thinking too hard about my self.

After building myself up from a heap of other people's thoughts and dreams, how shocking, then, to emerge into the stark fluorescent lights of an airport, to enter its crass brilliance, and discover I had no self, no one to define me. My plane ride to this new and foreign land of Albuquerque, New Mexico, was my first solitary journey, my first layover, my first disembarking. I got off the plane in a cold panic, lost. I frantically tried to disappear once again, to hide from the harsh light. Huddled between the shelves of an airport bookstore, I examined myself and found that I was empty. There was nothing there to see. Finally, the passage of time and the glare of the cashier ripped me from the grip of Nullity. Prompted by her look, I grabbed the cheapest, nearest book I could find. The book's weight in my hand was vaguely comforting.

In New Mexico, my book and I are left alone again. I spend the hot, bright days letting the glory of bone-white sidewalks burn away my pretensions towards identity. I play lightly with my voice, letting it flit and gravel-throat its way through stories and normal conversation. I experiment with the movement of my body, the inclination of my look. I discover I can be profound. I become outrageous, controversial, glinting glitter-bright fingernails every which way.

Two weeks later, my book and I leave New Mexico. I have memorized its cover: *The Hanged Man* by Francesca Lia Block. We travel onwards to New Orleans; its weight in my hands is again an anchor to reality.

In New Orleans, I am seduced by sepia, absorbed into a heaving mass of hued skin. I gladly lose myself in the balm of sweetly scented hair and cocoa butter. Here, again, I play with my identity. I leave my hair unrelaxed and wear it out. I learn to flash my eyes out – a coquette – and link arms with two girls I have befriended, the three of us ignoring the catcalls and hoots that track us down the street.

In New Mexico I discovered the desert night. I let its silence fill me and transform me until I am at once ethereal, eternal, serene. In New Orleans I learn to be strong. I am the one the dorm girls come to at night when the black sky has descended and someone has ordered pick-up chicken. I am the one known for being unafraid. By now, I have let my nails grow out, long and blunt, colored them a crimson red. Looking at them, I feel fierce, teeth blackened and filed to a point, like some old Mayan war story. I let my walk mime assertive strides.

It is hard to come home again, to once again surrender to the community of family, friends, and peers, whose needs and desires chafe and brush against the skin with a subtle, bitter susurrus. It is hard to return to school, to the daily routine. I feel sometimes as though the person who claimed mountains is no longer there.

But I try to remember this: the human soul is like a deck of tarot cards, and the mind is the dealer. Each card flipped is a facet of the potential self, each card a piece of a new person to be.

Maria I. Velazquez
Cambridge, Massachusetts 2005

*Maria studied philosophy and art history at Smith
College, and is now pursuing a master's degree
in gender and cultural studies at Simmons College.*

Damian Williams

Atlanta, Georgia 1998

WE WERE KNOWN AS "THA GANG"— THE
baddest group of eleven year olds on N.W.
Hamilton Terrace. Our covert missions took us all
over the world, from China (Chicken Eddie's
house) to Antarctica (my Aunt's kitchen). During
the day we ran from the perils of the African
wild (Nellie's old dog Fluffy), so at night we could
feast heartily (cheese pizza over Nintendo) and
dream of swimming in pristine waterfalls (the fire
hydrant at the corner). The summer of '91 was
all about exploration. We knew no limits. Living in
Harlem as a kid requires a vivid imagination;
it always seemed that the toys that we longed for
never came to our block. We had to improvise.

One particular day stands out clearly in my
memory of that summer. It was a Monday, and we
had traversed the world in a week, and decided
that outer space was far too complex to reach.
The group voted that a walk was in order, so we
set out on a journey to no particular place.
After about thirty minutes of crossing streets and
racking our brains for something to do, we
stumbled upon a nameless alley, ground sprinkled
with little glass vials with colored tops. Definitely
a game in the making.

We played everything with the tiny toys: catch
the "thingy," fire in the hole, and anything else we
thought possible. At the time, as far as we were
concerned, that day was like any other; in
retrospect, it shows something sad about reality.
Those vials were once filled with crack.

That summer was my only taste of Harlem,
and at the end of August I returned to my own
life, a world away from that New York block.
Sometimes, before going to sleep, we would sit on
the front stoop and talk about growing up to be
doctors and lawyers. It's funny how life works;
of the five of us, I am the only one who's still in
school. Two are in jail, and the others now
sell those little vials instead of playing with them.

Damian Williams
New Haven, Connecticut 2005

Damian studied economics at Harvard University,
and is now attending Yale Law School.

Anahad O'Connor

New York, New York 1999

EACH WEEKDAY, AS I ARRIVE IN MY neighborhood from school, I take notice of the disparity in population between the local library and the basketball courts. The library always appears scarcely populated. In contrast, the basketball courts are flooded with students recently let out of school. It occurred to me that most adolescents in my community see studying and schoolwork as a waste of their time. After pondering the reason behind this fallacy, I have concluded that these students lack role models and motivation.

There are relatively few college graduates living in my Lower East Side community. The small number who do graduate from college and begin a professional career usually leave for good. I feel that, as a minority, to turn my back on my community and move on would be a dereliction of moral duty.

As a senior in junior high school, I had little motivation to do well in school. Fortunately, with the help of my history teacher, Mrs. Bea, who believed and reposed confidence in me, I applied and was accepted to the Legal Outreach Program for high school students founded by Professor James B. O'Neil. Professor O'Neil, a graduate of Harvard University and one of Columbia University's few African-American professors, gave me the guidance and motivation that I needed to achieve success in high school. Professor O'Neil served as a much needed minority role model for me.

Through Legal Outreach's courses and internships in the field of the law I realized that I had great potential. There are many other minority students in my community with enormous potential and intellect. Unfortunately, they are lacking the minority role models and opportunities that I was so lucky to have.

After graduating from law school, Professor O'Neil decided to give back to the minority community that fostered him. As a result, my life was drastically changed for the better. To show my appreciation and gratitude, I must follow this paradigm and lead another misguided minority individual in the right direction.

After finishing school, I plan on returning to my neighborhood so that I can help other minority students follow in my footsteps. I would like to become a mentor to students who are, as I once was, bereft of the motivation and confidence necessary to do well in school. If I can lead at least one student away from a path of destruction and onto the road to a bright future, then I will have given back to my community.

It is not too much to ask that we, as minorities, promote education in our communities. Once black and Hispanic students see that they can use minority professionals – rather than athletes – as role-models, they will realize the significance of attaining an education. Only then will our youth be attracted to libraries instead of basketball courts.

Anahad O'Connor
New York, New York 2005

Anahad studied psychology at Yale University.
Now he is a reporter for The New York Times, *where*
he writes for the science and metro sections.

Nneka Madu

Dumfries, Virginia 2001

FOR AS LONG AS I CAN REMEMBER, MY favorite picture has been a group photo taken of my family and me with kids from my village on my first birthday party. Growing up, I loved this picture because I didn't have a lot of family in America, and it reminded me that I had people who loved me in Nigeria.

In the summer of seventh grade my mother took me back to visit Nigeria. I was really excited, and the first thing I wanted to do was meet the kids from my picture and find out what kind of people they had grown up to be. I was also a little anxious, worried that they would not remember me or like me.

It never crossed my mind to worry about whether or not they were all alive.

As it turned out, seven of the kids who attended my first birthday party did not live to see age thirteen. I was horrified. In all my years in America, no one I knew had ever died. Every friend I had made since second grade was still alive. So, I was even more horrified to learn that they died of diarrhea, measles, and fever.

My mother, who is a nurse, spent the rest of the trip explaining to me the conditions in our village. We visited sick children, and she showed me the hospitals that were available to them. The closest hospital is miles away, in Owere. No one in the village owns a car, so when someone gets sick they have to be taken into town on a motorcycle. Many mothers cannot take the time away from farming to go to the city for inoculations, and those that can have no way of getting there.

I found the situation heartbreaking. I had always thought that I wanted to go into medicine, but that trip really made it my goal. When I am 30 and, by God's grace, out of medical school, I hope to go back and open a small clinic on the border between two neighboring villages and my own.

Given unlimited resources, I would set up an infant and childhood care program for these three villages. We would start by paving an emergency route between my clinic and the hospital in Owere so that during rainy season a muddy road will not prevent anyone from receiving medical help. Two vans would transport injured and sick people in each village.

A nurse and pharmacist would live in each village, answer health-related questions, and counsel new mothers on controlling diarrhea and treating ear infections. The pharmacist would be able to dispense free medicine prescribed in the hospital or the clinic. Those working in the clinic would go into the villages four times a year to offer free inoculations against childhood diseases; the clinic would also offer free check-ups. We would also try to dig, filter, or irrigate a clean water source for each village, and create an educational program to teach school children disease control, first aid, and AIDS education.

For five years, I would keep data on the cases treated, the mistakes made along the way, and the improvements needed for the program. This would lead to a more efficient model of a program for people to reproduce in their own villages. With the help of others, the program's short term goal would be to decrease infant and childhood mortality rates in my village and neighboring villages; the long term goal would be to lower childhood mortality in all of Nigeria and around the world.

This would benefit the parents of children living in a Third World country, and any child who has lost a playmate along the way.

Nneka Madu
New Haven, Connecticut 2005

Nneka studied history of science and medicine at Yale University. Now she works at the Glencree Centre for Reconciliation in Wicklow, Ireland, a non-governmental organization that works to identify gaps and fulfill needs in the peace-building process.

Gerald "Jay" Williams

Buffalo, New York 1999

"He gets excellent grades, he's an athlete, he's active in his church, he's the only student in City Honors history to be elected Student Council President as a junior, he's an asset to his community. Every student should be like him." They – my friends, my educators, my associates – often see my face, but not my heart. They say I am . . . But this is who I am:

I live on the East Side, B.K.A. (better known as) *the ghetto.* It is almost entirely composed of people of color, and the economic deficiencies are obvious. Money is tight, and the maxim "It's not what you eat, it's *if* you eat" is heard far too often.

I can vividly recall the night when my family was awakened by a gunshot – a bullet entered our window. No one was physically injured, but mentally and emotionally this small object pierced our hearts. I have often been asked, "Why doesn't your family move to a better part of town?" With pride I can respond that my church, my school, my family, and my people are in my neighborhood, components of my life on which I shall never turn my back.

When Granny died on January 20, 1998, I was pretty sure our family would be largely altered. Still, we are all together. Granny left a mark on her community as a caring neighbor, a loving Christian, and a Boy Scout den mother. Most deeply, she left a mark on her family, which has grown due to the need to fill the void left by her passing. The apartment upstairs from mine is now empty, but my heart is overflowing. Her caring spirit taught me how to grow and how to always keep God and family a priority in my life. They say I am . . . a family man . . . I say I am nothing without family.

They say I am . . . But in the words of renowned African-American author Toni Morrison, "Their description does not fit my tongue." I cannot be summarized through some accomplishment or deed. I do not need to prevent a war or save the rain forest, but by continually supporting my neighborhood, my roots, I can change the world.

The ghetto believed in me, and I believe in the ghetto.

I am unable to definitively recite the history of my family – lost in the passage, lost in the slavery, lost in the battle. I can say, however, where my family, my people, and I are going: We're going onward. I love my neighborhood. It may be violent and at times very scary, but it raised and protected me.

They say I am a hardworking student . . . a religious teenager . . . a dedicated family man . . . a black male. I not only say I am, but I *know* I am a believer. I believe in my church, my school, and my family. I believe in my neighborhood and my people. I cannot turn my back. I am . . .

Gerald "Jay" Williams
New York, New York 2005

Jay received a bachelor's degree in the comparative
study of religion from Harvard University.
He is now an assistant vice president with the private
banking group of Merrill Lynch in New York.

Jamaal Anthony Young

Columbia, South Carolina 1999

LEARNING HOW TO LOVE ONE'S SELF IS perhaps one of the most difficult hurdles to over-come. It is an inner battle between self-doubt and self-confidence, intolerance and appreciation. It is a struggle to accept those strengths and weaknesses that define character. Often, we attempt to hide those character-building attributes in order to conform to some larger whole. But perhaps it is best to recognize those differences that set us apart from the crowd. It has taken me years of personal growth in order to come to this realization, but it has been a worthwhile evolution. I have learned to value all aspects of myself – my past, my present, and my potential.

It is commonly believed that ignorance is bliss, and as a child, I was quite happy. Until the age of six, I lived only with my mother and my German grandmother in a small Kansas neighborhood. I was unaware of the fact that I had no father and that I was multiracial. I never questioned where my father was, or why my mother was so "light-skinned." Like most children, in my early years I was perfectly content. I remember my grand-mother singing German lullabies to me when I had a nightmare; I remember thinking that my mother was the most beautiful woman in the world.

When I was six years old, my mother married a man who was in the Army, and shortly afterwards my mother, my new father, and I moved to Germany. The three years spent in my Oma's native land are the childhood experiences that have most vividly affected me. Interacting with the German culture was not at all difficult, especially considering the heavy influence of my grand-mother. I remember the language, the everyday customs, and especially the food. Vacations took my family and me to the October Fest in Munich, historic Nuremberg, and the scenic beauty of the Rhine. These experiences fostered my love and appreciation for all cultural differences.

Yet, after our time in Europe we moved back to America, and I learned that others did not hold cultural differences in the same regard. In Louisiana and Alabama I experienced a new form of cultural behavior – racism. Because of my mixed heritage, I was marked as an outsider by both the Caucasian and African-American communities. As a result, I developed a general mistrust for others. Due in part to these trials, I experienced a lack of self-confidence that prevented me from interacting with my peers.

That continued until about the age of 14, while we were living in Texas. For years there had been external pressure to pick a side – either I would be black or I would be white. It was then that I decided to no longer allow the whims of a closed-minded society to dictate my actions or my happiness. I would not be labeled a "sell-out" by the African-American community because I competed in the mostly white field of speech and debate. Nor would I be considered the token black in student council by the Caucasian population. I would not be a smart black man, nor a smart white man, but an intelligent person regardless of my heritage. I would not learn conformity but, rather, to regain that appreciation of uniqueness so prevalent in my childhood. I have turned those conditions that were once a weakness into a strength.

I still have more challenges to master during my journey of personal development, but I am comfortable with where my life is now. The battle between insecurity and confidence has been won. My heritage is no longer a source of discomfort, but of pride and confidence. I look forward to a future where my past and present experiences will help me be successful. I have learned to love and accept others, but most importantly, to love and accept myself.

Jamaal Anthony Young
Washington, D.C. 2005

Jamaal studied culture and politics at Georgetown University. He works in the Washington office of City Year, a national service organization and think-tank, as national mobilization coordinator.

Sparlha Swa

Oyster Bay, New York 1997

How we look at the road stretched before us has a huge impact on what we see. Ever searching for potholes and fallen trees will only extend to these obstacles a warmer, less resistible invitation. On the other hand, if one looks down that same road with eyes pealed for the positive, then something wonderful will appear – bright treasures hiding in the bushes, amazing souls soon to approach. Thus, in order to live most contentedly, yet without denial, in a world full of want, inequality, and struggle, it is essential to be able to understand and reform the way we perceive it; put simply, to be optimistic.

The people I believe would benefit most from this positive outlook are the poor, those who are confronted on a daily basis with conditions both deplorable and self-perpetuating. To help accomplish this, I would open a free daycare center or a Boys and Girls Club-type organization, since the easiest way to integrate a way of thinking into a person's life is to expose them to it at an early age. There, hassle-free from whatever problems they might be facing at home or school, children could get a free meal, take refuge in the program, and engage in educational group activities in which my ideas could be conveyed.

First, I would show them how to recognize and cultivate their own special talents, how to appreciate themselves. Centering on the arts, the program would foster an atmosphere that nurtures creativity and self-expression. This would in turn encourage better communication – and thereby better interaction with others – and develop skills that might eventually be the force to propel them from their economic straits. I would also introduce them to the wonderful morals of Shel Silverstein and Dr. Suess, two children's authors that aim, simply, to share with their readers some of the marvels of life. Showing poor children the value and beauty in themselves would make it easier for them to find more of the same in situations and people encountered later on.

Equipped with the force of optimism, one's troubles become gentle lessons, the withered dust of malnourished dreams transforms into fertile earth, vitalizing the new. Firm in the belief that storm clouds herald greener grass, a smile is suddenly worth a thousand more, and the cold of winter serves to make one's blankets that much warmer. When one sees the glass as half-full, and the difficult road awaiting them as an adventure, then life becomes a blessing, as it should be.

Sparlha Swa
New York, New York 2005

Sparlha studied anthropology at Stanford University.
She is a singer and songwriter based in New York.

Carmelle T. Norice

Los Angeles, California 1997

A MAJOR EXPERIENCE IN MY LIFE THAT HAS shaped my values, ethical positions, community involvement, and goals is the incarceration of a very close and dear member of my family, who, under the influence of a mind-altering drug to which he was severely addicted, committed a series of non-fatal crimes for which he presently serves a life sentence under the "Three-Strikes" law.

The incarceration of my family member has caused me levels of grief and pain that I cannot even begin to articulate. It has also, however, caused me to view the incarceration of other individuals in similar cases in a different light. My values and ethical positions are, in large part, a result of this enlightened perspective.

Through this major life experience, I have come to suspect that there is less humaneness and ethicality behind our incarceration of this class of offenders than we realize. The majority of society, myself included, believes that crime should not go uncorrected; criminals should not go unpunished. Such corrections are an obvious requisite for the maintenance of an orderly and safe society. Through this major experience of my life I have come to believe, however, that with every judgment of crimes committed under the influence of mind-altering drugs, there is a criminal – a "partner-in-crime", if you will – that we let go unpunished: drug addiction. A just judgment divides the punishment between this undercover offender and the human criminal.

Seeing that much of the time being served by thousands across the land is due to this undercover criminal, I have thus been inspired to help *uncover* it and its deeds, so that we can give "the human criminals" more appropriate sentences. After graduating with a bachelor's degree in neuroscience, I plan to become a student of a distinguished M.D./Ph.D. program that will adequately prepare me to become a psychiatrist and neuropharmacologist. I also want to become a Christian minister. I believe that with these fields of expertise, I will be able to make profound investigations into the effects of mind-altering drug addiction. Hopefully, my contributions will help make our judgments of criminal cases more just.

In light of "punishing" drug addiction, I plan to co-design drug rehabilitation centers for offenders whose crimes were committed under the influence of mind-altering drugs. Drawing upon my knowledge and expertise, as well as those of others desiring to make a difference in the lives of many, the rehabilitation centers would offer the most effective forms of treatment possible. If, as I hope, the drug rehabilitation centers are sponsored by the U.S. government, perhaps a significant number of offenders would be permitted to serve an appropriate amount of their time there. In actuality, however, it would be the time during which the drug addiction would serve *its* time, and, hopefully, be *executed* as well.

The incarceration of my family member has been both a destructive and constructive force in my life: destructive in the way it has physically separated me from someone to whom I am strongly attached; constructive in the way it has revolutionized my perspective and positions on incarceration and been a large source of inspiration for my future goals. Having had, for myself, a taste of the bitter injustices being done to certain criminals and their loved ones across this land, I am now convinced that something major must be done to convince the cook that he needs a new recipe. For being thus convinced, I am thankful to God for this experience, and believe that it will ultimately be for the betterment of humanity.

Carmelle T. Norice
New York, New York 2005

*Carmelle studied molecular, cellular and developmental
biology at the University of California, Los Angeles.
She is enrolled in the Medical Scientist Training
Program at Columbia University. She plans to pursue
biomedical research in the area of infectious diseases.*

Myia A. Alston

Washington, D.C. 1997

IF I COULD SPEND ONE EVENING WITH A person I admire, I would have to spend it with Terina Alston, my mother.

Because this evening would probably be a once-in-a-lifetime event, most people would probably choose someone they have never met, or a celebrity of some kind. That is why I would spend it with my mother. I have not lived with her since I was in eighth grade, and I can count on both hands the number of times I have seen her since our separation.

Until a month ago, my mother was a heavy substance abuser. She did not use prescription drugs, but illegal substances. She used to be unbearable, unapproachable, and an unfit parent.

Now, however, things are changing. She lives in a women's shelter and is receiving drug counseling.

This is why I admire her: she is doing what many of her old drug partners cannot do – she is cleaning herself up after nearly twenty years as a substance abuser.

During our evening together, she would cook me dinner, something she has not done in years. Then, during our meal, we would talk about all the things we never could during our thirteen years together, and I would update her on all the things she has missed in the last four years.

This evening would be one of the most special times I have ever had. I would take the time to tell my mother that I have forgiven her for all the pain she has caused me. I would also let her know that I want her to continue to get herself together because she is not physically strong enough to abuse her body anymore.

If this evening came to pass, my mother and I would talk all night. I would tell her over and over again that she is the person I most admire. And, I would tell her to keep up her strength so that I can follow her example of being wise enough to give up the things that are harmful, and strong enough to take on those that are tough but necessary.

Myia A. Alston
New York, New York 2005

Myia graduated from George Washington University with a degree in electronic media, and studied radio, television and film at Syracuse University. Now she is Manager of Media Planning and Music Video Production and Acquisitions for Nickelodeon Digital Cable Networks in New York. Myia's mother died two weeks after Myia wrote her essay, and she never got to have the dinner she wanted. On the day she wrote her essay, however, she visited her mother at the women's shelter where she was living, and she told her she loved her. It was the last time she saw her alive.

Eric S. Teasley

Inglewood, California 2003

THE BUS STOP IS ONLY FIFTEEN MINUTES away, but it takes an hour and a half to get there. After rolling out of an inadequate sleep, waiting for the family to cycle through the shower, and inhaling a bowl of corn flakes, I'm left with those fifteen minutes to negotiate the early morning streets of Inglewood.

There is no room for error. Punctuality ultimately depends on the caprices of Interstate 405, which is more of a merciless monster than an essential thoroughfare. Massive and serpentine, it growls with characteristic highway roar as it snakes its way through the concrete canyons of Los Angeles. With a heartless accident, a pitiless on-ramp meter, or any distraction off to the shoulder, the interstate decides whether I, in a car, reach my bus stop, or get stuck behind a mess that Caltrans will ignore until we are all sufficiently late for our lives.

The bus, meanwhile, is never affected by these woes. Somehow it manages to roll merrily on its way, perfectly on time. It parts the waters of slowly flowing traffic as if its bright yellow glow were some divine light. And that is why the bus stop causes domestic disturbances. If I do not reach the usual stop, then I must be driven to the next. This adds ten more minutes of school bus-catching to mom's commute, and undoubtedly ten more minutes of her exasperated screaming, and eventually ten more minutes of her boss's exasperated screaming. In those ten minutes I can have ten brushes with death, not only at the hands of the banshee in the driver's seat, but also every law-abiding motorist we whoosh past in pursuit of that distant yellow dot. The circle of strife continues further, with ten more minutes of heated discussion, once the bus returns from a tough day of school at seven in the evening. Like the epicenter of a Southland quake, the bus stop can radiate wrath into all aspects of weekday life. Aftershocks continue to rattle my sanity.

The bus stop plots against me. As if to punish those who are late, the bus stop might decide to summon all the evil, identical bus minions and dispatch them into the streets to bring false hope to stragglers. It is quite unsettling when one catches the wrong bus and realizes that the right bus is God-only-knows how far in the distance. An unusually long series of busses, each grinning with shiny steel grills, might cross the intersection ahead, each one mocking me as mom censors her cursing at a red light with periodic beeps of the horn. At that point I usually turn my head to the window and try to focus on something else. If I'm lucky, I might see another late family, a mother on the verge of eating her offspring, also stuck in the parking lot that is the weekday commute.

But reaching the bus stop – and the bus – after the adrenaline rush of the morning is not unlike achieving Nirvana. Not only does it end the journey, but it also liberates me, for at least an hour, from the petty difficulties of morning life. The rickety vibrations of the bus have a way of lulling me into deep meditation, and as I philosophically gaze out the windows, I reflect on as many topics as are mirrored by the tinted glass.

As the bus shuttles me out of the ghetto and into the world of private school, I ponder the huge disparity between where I live and where I learn. I examine the contrast between the chaos that just ended and the contentment of the place I'm headed, where the most urgent crisis of the moment is "like, whatever." Yes, where I live and where I learn are as different as black and white, and at times the difference is overwhelming. The bus stop is the intermediary between these two parallel universes, located almost perfectly on the Los Angeles color line.

The bus stop, however, is a sacrifice I am willing to make. Chances are that I would not even be writing this essay were it not for the bus stop and the school that provides it. In that sense, I am extremely indebted to the bus service, and my family is extremely indebted to the bank because of the outrageous charge that service entails. I doubt the service has any idea how much impact its daily journey has had on this one customer.

That favorite childhood song never rang clearer in my mind than when I was in high school: the wheels on the bus really do go round and round, round and round, round and round, no matter who is desperately trailing behind them.

Eric S. Teasley
Stanford, California 2005

Eric studies chemical engineering at Stanford University. He is relieved that his days chasing school buses are over.

Ron Brown Scholars

1997–2005

Myia A. Alston *(p.106)*
Washington, D.C.
College George Washington University
Major Electronic Media
Graduate Program Syracuse University
Employment Nickelodeon Digital Networks,
New York, NY

Michael Billings
Salt Lake City, Utah
College The Wharton School,
University of Pennsylvania
Major Economics
Concentration Management
Employment Coatue Management, New York, NY

Jordan C. Brewer
Los Angeles, California
College School of Engineering,
Massachusetts Institute of Technology
Major Computer Science
Employment Hewlett Packard, San Diego, CA

John Alexander Burton
Miami, Florida
College Harvard University
Major History and Literature
Employment The Center for American Progress,
Washington, D.C.

Terence Carter
Chevy Chase, Maryland
College Harvard University
Major Affrican-American Studies
Employment NBC Television, Hollywood, CA

Yolanda Covington-Ward
Ann Arbor, Michigan
College Brown University
Major Affrican-American Studies
Graduate Program University of Michigan,
Ann Arbor

Kelly Cross
Beckley, West Virginia
College Princeton University
Major German
Graduate Program University of Virginia
Law School
Employment Patton Boggs LLP, Washington, D.C.

Megan C. M. Donovan
Washington, D.C.
College Harvard University
Major Economics
Employment Filene's, Boston, Massachusetts

Marco F. Ellis
Manassas, Virginia
College University of Virginia
Major Biochemistry
Graduate Program Harvard University
Medical School
Employment Northwestern University
Medical Center, Chicago, IL

Travis A. Gayles
Chase City, Virginia
College Duke University
Major Public Policy; African-American
Studies, Certificate in Health Policy
Graduate Program University of Illinois
Medical School

Bianca Kannatey-Asibu
Ann Arbor, Michigan
College Stanford University
Major Architecture/Urban Studies

Diarra K. Lamar
Montgomery, Alabama
College Harvard University
Major Cognitive Neuroscience
Graduate Programs Harvard University Medical
School; Harvard University Business School

Angela Ledbetter
Detroit, Michigan
College Xavier University of Louisiana
Major Chemistry
Graduate Program Wayne State University
Medical School
Employment St. John Hospital, Detroit, Michigan

Carmelle T. Norice *(p.104)*
Los Angeles, California
College University of California – Los Angeles
Major Molecular, Cellular, and
Developmental Biology
Graduate Program Columbia University
Medical Scientist Training Program (MD/PhD)

M. Michelle Robinson
McLean, Virginia
College Harvard University
Major English and American Language
and Literature
Graduate Program Harvard University
Divinity School, Boston University
Graduate School

Kelli Stewart
Bartlett, Tennessee
College Emory University
Major Economics and Education
Graduate Program New York University
School of Law
Employment Entrepreneur

F. Anthony St. Louis
Rosedale, New York
College Massachusetts Institute of Technology
Major Computer Science and Electrical Engineering
Employment Vermont Telephone Company, Chester, Vt.

Sparlha Swa (p.102)
Oyster Bay, New York
College Stanford University
Major Anthropology
Employment Singer, Songwriter, New York, NY

J. Paulson Tuffet *(p.68)*
Miami, Florida
College University of Pennsylvania
Major Economics and Political Science
Graduate Program Georgetown University School of Law

Luther Williams
Oakland, California
College Harvard University
Major Government
Employment Maverick Capital, LTD, New York, NY

1998

Elizabeth V. Alicea
Chicago, Illinois
College Columbia University
Major Sociology
Employment Advantage Testing, Inc., New York, NY

Jennifer Marie Banner
New York, New York
College Harvard University
Major Government
Graduate Program University of Virginia School of Law
Employment Mayor, Brown, Rowe & Maw, LLP, New York, NY

Traci R. Burch
Bear, Delaware
College Princeton University
Major Politics
Graduate Program Harvard University

Shirley Delaleu
Elmont, New York
College Stanford University
Major Human Biology
Graduate Program Mount Sinai Medical School

Maleka Donaldson Gramling
Columbus, Ohio
College Harvard University
Major Biology
Employment ASAFO Media, Washington, D.C.

Melanie Lynette Forbes
Midlothian, Virginia
College Harvard University
Major Social Studies
Graduate Program Harvard University Law School

Tiffany Y. Griswell
Columbus, North Carolina
College University of North Carolina, Chapel Hill
Major Business Administration
Employment SunTrust Bank, Atlanta, GA

Antonia J. Henry *(p.48)*
Grand Rapids, Michigan
College University of Michigan
Major Microbiology
Graduate Program Harvard University Medical School

Leah Hodge
Jacksonville, Florida
College The Wharton School, University of Pennsylvania
Major Accounting, *Minor* Hispanic Studies
Graduate Program Stanford Graduate School of Business

Christopher Anthony Hunter
Los Angeles, California
College Harvard University
Major Literature
Graduate Program University of Pennsylvania

Fatime Kaba
New York, New York
College Columbia University
Major African-American Studies
Employment New Line Cinema, New York, NY

Marc Q. Knight
Elmont, New York
College Massachusetts Institute of Technology
Major Electrical Engineering and Computer Science/Management Science
Graduate Program Massachusetts Institute of Technology
Employment Morgan Stanley, New York, NY

Tiombe E. C. Jones Osisanya
Palmdale, California
College Pomona College
Major Sociology
Graduate Program Loyola Law School

Jonathan Piper
University Heights, Ohio
College Wake Forest University
Major Chemistry
Graduate Program Wake Forest University

Tomeka Suber
Greensboro, North Carolina
College University of North Carolina,
Chapel Hill
Major Chemistry, *Minor:* African
American Studies
Graduate Program Johns Hopkins Medical School

Sara Whetstone
Palo Alto, California
College Brown University
Major Community Health
Graduate Program Yale University Medical
School

Aaliyah Williams
Tulsa, Oklahoma
College Harvard University
Major Psychology
Employment American Express, New York, NY

Damian Williams *(p.92)*
Stone Mountain, Georgia
College Harvard University
Major Economics
Graduate Program Cambridge University,
Yale University Law School

Tracy M. Wynter
Willingboro, New Jersey
College Princeton University
Major Economics
Graduate Program Temple University Law School

Allen Yancy
Baltimore, Maryland
College Harvard University
Major History
Graduate Program Yale University Law School

1999

Martine Caverl
Richton Park, Illinois
College New York University
Major Cultural Anthropology
Employment Block Together, Chicago, IL

Morgan K. Dooley *(p.24)*
Atlanta, Georgia
College Emory University
Major Anthropology and Human Biology
Graduate Program Emory University Graduate
School; Johns Hopkins Medical School

Kyla Dotson
Biloxi, Mississippi
College Williams College
Major Anthropology
Employment Government Agency,
Washington, D.C.

Matthew Espy
Decatur, Georgia
College Harvard University
Major Applied Mathematics
Employment Bridgewater Associates, Westport, CT

Derick Gross *(p.52)*
Greenlawn, New York
College Columbia University
Major Engineering
Employment Rainbow Chimes Early Childhood
and Care Center, New York, NY

Katori Hall *(p.32)*
Memphis, Tennessee
College Columbia University
Major African-American Studies and
Creative Writing
Graduate Program Harvard University Master
of Fine Arts Program

Kara P. Hamilton
Brooklyn, New York
College Harvard University
Major Government
Graduate Program London School of Economics
and Political Science

Tiffany R. Jackson
Bryan, Texas
College Harvard University
Major Biochemical Sciences
Graduate Program Harvard University
Medical School

Charly Jeune
Los Angeles, California
College Massachusetts Institute of Technology
Major Electrical Engineering
Employment Horace Mann Junior High School,
Los Angeles, CA

Gwendolyn Jones
Wichita, Kansas
College University of Texas – Austin
Major Finance
Employment Beazer Homes, Atlanta, GA

Nakiya K. Jones *(p.18)*
Dallas, Texas
College University of Texas – Austin
Major Government and Journalism
Employment ACORN Organization,
Oakland, CA

Lanakila "Ku" McMahan
High Point, North Carolina
College Duke University
Major Environmental Science and Policy
Graduate Program University of North
Carolina – Chapel Hill

"The Ron Brown
Scholarship has been
far more than just
a means to pay for my
higher education.
More importantly,
everyone involved in
the program has been
like a family to me,
particularly during my
time at University
of Virginia Law School
in Charlottesville.
The support, love, and
genuine concern
shown to me thus far
touches my heart and
I feel truly blessed to
have such thoughtful,
kind-hearted, and
wonderful people in
my corner. The great-
est benefit is being
able to interact with
other Ron Brown
Scholars who have
overcome many
obstacles in their lives
to do such extraordi-
nary things. I look
forward to sharing
more wisdom,
interesting experiences,
and fun times with
everyone in the Ron
Brown Scholar family
as we try to make
the world a better
place. Thanks so much
to the CAP Charitable
Foundation for
making such an
important impact on
my life; my only wish
is that they will be
proud – of what I
have done and what I
know they have faith
I will do in the future."

Jennifer Marie Banner
1998 Ron Brown Scholar

Sean Nolan
Valrico, Florida
College Massachusetts Institute of Technology
Major Aerospace Engineering
Graduate Program Massachusetts Institute of Technology

Anahad O'Connor *(p.94)*
New York, New York
College Yale University
Major Psychology
Employment The New York Times, New York, NY

Ernest Scott
Houston, Texas
College Howard University
Major Finance
Employment Goldman Sachs & Co., New York, NY

Dorothy Loretta Ann Smith *(p.44)*
Dallas, Texas
College Harvard University
Major Sociology
Employment DC Appleseed Center for Law and Justice, Inc., Washington, D.C.

Ryan A. Stewart
Arlington, Texas
College Stanford University
Major Economics
Employment Teach for America, Palo Alto, CA

Gerald "Jay" Williams *(p.98)*
Buffalo, New York
College Harvard University
Major Comparative Study of Religion
Employment Merrill Lynch, New York, NY

Nneka Williams
New York, New York
College Harvard University
Major Earth and Planetary Sciences
Employment Schlumberger Oil Field Services Company, Malaysia

Jamaal Anthony Young *(p.100)*
Columbia, South Carolina
College Georgetown University
Major Culture and Politics
Employment City Year, Washington, D.C.

2000

Amanda S. Alexander
Plainwell, Michigan
College Harvard University
Major Government and African Studies
Employment Centre for Civil Society, Durban, South Africa

S. Michael Anderson
Pheonix, Arizona
College Arizona State University
Major Microbiology

Kolade Apata
Fayetteville, Georgia
College Emory University
Major Computer Science and Finance
Employment The Boston Consulting Group, Atlanta, GA

T. J. Berrings
Waterbury, Vermont
College Stanford University
Major Human Thought
Employment D. E. Shaw & Co., Cupertino, CA

Jamar Campbell *(p.80)*
Aurora, Colorado
College Northwestern University
Major Economics and Political Science
Employment Kaplan, Inc.

Lauren M. Goins
Gretna, Louisiana
College Harvard University
Major Biochemical Sciences
Graduate Program University of California, San Francisco

Tristan D. Ivory
Oxnard, California
College Stanford University
Major Comparative Studies in Race and Ethnicity
Graduate Program University of California, Los Angeles

Ilisten M. Jones *(p.84)*
Carson, California
College Harvard University
Major Biochemical Sciences
Graduate Program Harvard University Medical School

Julian M. Jordan
Fort Wayne, Indiana
College Brown University
Major International Relations
Employment Merrill Lynch, New York, NY

Kara M. Lee
Uniondale, New York
College Harvard University
Major Biomedical Engineering
Graduate Program Hofstra University

May Lorna Lugemwa
Birmingham, Alabama
College Harvard University
Major Visual and Environmental Studies (Film) and Sociology
Employment Filmmaker, Los Angeles, CA

Eddie Martin
Northport, Alabama
College Mississippi State University
Major International Business

Donielle N. Newell
Naperville, Illinois
College Stanford University
Major Biomechanical Engineering
Graduate Program Stanford University

Marques J. Redd
Macon, Georgia
Major Social Studies and African and
African-American Studies
Graduate Program University of California,
Berkeley

Petra M. Sander
Amherst, Massachussetts
College Princeton University
Major Molecular Biology
Employment Teach for America, Miami, FL

Angela A. Smedley *(p.88)*
Ann Arbor, Michigan
College Harvard University
Major Sociology and African-American Studies
Employment Wilkie, Farr & Gallagher, LLP

Joni C. Stuart
Stuarts Draft, Virginia
College Xavier University – Louisiana
Major Biology, *Minor:* Chemistry
Graduate Program VCU, Medical College
of Virginia

Maria I. Velazquez *(p.90)*
Springfield, Massachusetts
College Smith College
Major Philosophy, *Minor:* Art History
Graduate Program Simmons College

Courtney Wooten
Oakland, California
College Stanford University
Major Sociology
Employment Freelance Writer, Everett, WA

Jason W. Young
Inglewood, California
College Harvard University
Major Economics
Employment Merrill Lynch, Plainsboro, NJ

2001

Sheila Adams
Bronx, New York
College Harvard University
Major Sociology
Service Abroad Michael C. Rockefeller
Memorial Fellowship Recipient, Brazil

Eleanor Branch
Sacramento, California
College Stanford University
Major Earth Systems
Graduate Program Stanford University

Robert Lee Brutus III
Bronx, New York
College Princeton University
Major Classics

William S. Chichester III
Warrenton, Virginia
College University of Virginia
Major Foreign Relations and Middle
Eastern Studies
Employment The Vanguard Group,
Philadelphia, PA.

Victor A. Davis *(p.72)*
Washington, D.C.
College Princeton University
Major Economics
Employment Accenture, New York, NY

Caleb Franklin *(p.46)*
Los Angeles, California
College Harvard University
Major Social Studies
Film Study Gardner Fellowship, Mumbai
(Bombay), India

Karla J. Hardy
Tyler, Texas
College Iowa State University
Major Business Management and
International Business
Employment Council on African American Affairs,
Washington, D.C.

Morgan G. Harper *(p.82)*
Columbus, Ohio
College Tufts University
Major Community Health and Spanish
Employment Federal Trade Commission,
Washington, D.C.

Brennan D. Johnson
Des Moines, Iowa
College Grinnell College
Major Philosophy and Linguistics
Employment Lenox Manufacturing,
Marshalltown, IA

Maris Jones
El Cerrito, California
College Stanford University
Major Human Biology
Graduate Program University of Illinois,
Chicago School of Medicine

"Being selected as
a Ron Brown Scholar
has been one of my
life's biggest
blessings. Becoming
a Scholar not only
awarded me the
financial security
necessary to achieve
one of my academic
goals, but also
connected me to a
broader network
of people who are
committed to over-
coming obstacles,
to personal excellence,
and to affecting
positive social change
in our communities.
As I reflect on
the opportunity that
the CAP Charitable
Foundation so gra-
ciously made possible,
I am only further
impassioned to extend
to others the
possibilities planted
in me."

Dorothy Loretta Ann Smith
1999 Ron Brown Scholar

Christopher Khan
Silver Spring, Maryland
College Northwestern University
Major Industrial Engineering, Political Science,
International Studies
Concentration Business Management
Employment U.S. Marine Corps –
Military Intelligence

Nneka Madu *(p.96)*
Dumfries, Virginia
College Yale University
Major Psychology
Service Abroad Glencree Centre for
Reconciliation, Dublin, Ireland

Khalia Mounsey
Baltimore, Maryland
College Duke University
Major Public Policy Studies
Employment May Tech Corporation,
Silver Spring, MD

Misha M. Mutizwa *(p.78)*
Rocky River, Ohio
Major Public Policy Studies,
Concentration Health Policy
College Duke University
Graduate Program Duke University Medical
School

Brandon L. Nicholson *(p.16)*
Oakland, California
College Princeton University
Major Public Policy
Graduate Program University of California –
Berkeley

Saundra S. Quinlan
Laurelton, New York
College Massachusetts Institute of Technology
Major Mechanical Engineering
Minor African Diaspora Studies
Employment Accenture, Atlanta, GA

Dylan Solomon
San Diego, California
College Stanford University
Major Electrical Engineering
Employment Quantum Secure, San Jose, CA

Michael Thompson
Bronx, New York
College Harvard University
Major Government and African-American Studies
Graduate Program Harvard University Law School

Veronica H. Threadgill *(p.74)*
Brooklyn, New York
College Roger Williams University
Major Accounting, Financial Services
Minor Math
Employment KPMG, New York, NY

Koryse S. Woodrooffe
Brooklyn, New York
College Vanderbilt University
Major Biological Science
Graduate Program Albert Einstein College
of Medicine

DeLeon Wright
Long Island City, New York
College Amherst College
Major Theatre
Employment Teach for America, Chicago, IL

2002

Danielle C. Andrews-Lovell
Miami, Florida
College Harvard University
Major Biochemistry

Tamika Bailey
Miami, Florida
College Northwestern University
Major Psychology
Graduate Program Northwestern Feinberg
School of Medicine

Jade Alexander Craig
Hattiesburg, Mississippi
College University of Virginia
Major French and Political and Social Thought

Ghideon Z. Ezaz
Piney Woods, Mississippi
College Washington University – St. Louis
Major Biomedical Engineering

Immanuel R. Foster *(p.30)*
Berkeley, California
College Harvard University
Major Physics and Chemistry

James French
Mt. Vernon, New York
College Harvard University
Major Classical Studies

Alem Giorgis
Lawrenceville, Georgia
College Yale University
Major African Studies and Political Science

Lisa Gordon
Miramar, Florida
College Harvard University
Major Sociology and African-American Studies

Ashley Hayes
Atlanta, Georgia
College Columbia University
Major East Asian Studies

Alvin Ellsworth Hough Jr.
Washington, D.C.
College Harvard University
Major Earth and Planetary Sciences

Amanda K. Johnson
Milwaukee, Wisconsin
College Stanford University
Major Human Biology and Spanish

Luis Jones
Eufaula, Alabama
College Stanford University
Major Biomechanical Engineering

Jacquelin S. King
Philadelphia, Pennsylvania
College University of Pennsylvania
Majors African Studies, English,
Urban Education

Marquise J. McGraw *(p.58)*
Bronx, New York
College Cornell University
Major Economics

Ijah Mondesire-Crump
Bronx, New York
College Harvard University
Major Biology

Tracy Moore
Cincinnati, Ohio
College Harvard University
Concentration Classics

Kalonji L. K. Nzinga
Columbus, Ohio
College Stanford University
Major Human Biology

Errol C. Saunders II *(p.86)*
Covina, California
College Yale University
Major Political Science

Lordserious J. Watson *(p.50)*
Stone Mountain, Georgia
College Georgia Tech University
Major Engineering

Ellen Tachiewaa Yiadom *(p.54)*
Chicago, Illinois
College Harvard University
Major Government and French

2003

Ihotu J. Ali *(p.40)*
Minnetonka, Minnesota
College Macalester College
Major International Studies and Sociology

Autumn Joy Anderson *(p.66)*
Berkeley, California
College University of California – Berkeley
Major African-American Studies,
Rhetoric and Sociology

Stefon Q. Burns
White Plains, Maryland
College University of Pennsylvania –
Wharton School
Major Economics

Brandon L. Cook *(p.76)*
Dulles, Virginia
College Yale University
Major Linguistics

Wendy F. Francois *(p.22)*
Naranja, Florida
College Columbia University
Major Political Science and Human Rights

Jennifer N. Green
Louisville, Kentucky
College Harvard University
Major Government

Daphra A. Holder
Brooklyn, New York
College Princeton University
Major Political Science

Sarah Beverly LaBrie
Houston, Texas
College Brown University
Major Comparative Literature

Jessica Larché *(p.42)*
Gretna, Louisiana
College Florida A&M University
Major Broadcast Journalism

Kelly L. Lee *(p.12)*
Springfield, Oregon
College Simmons College
Major Sociology and Africana Studies

Yann G. Le Gall
Pittsburgh, Pennsylvania
College Princeton University
Major Chemical Engineering

Ivy M. McCottry
Philadelphia, Pennsylvania
College Cornell University
Major Urban and Regional Studies

Danielle McCullough
Baltimore, Maryland
College Harvard University
Major Psychology

"The day I received
the Ron Brown
Scholarship was a
seminal event and
turning point in
my life. Unlike other
accolades I received,
RBS served as a
rocket, launching me
to new heights.
Propelled with forti-
tude, RBS continues
to allow me to
overcome the seem-
ingly insurmountable
and achieve the
inaccessible. I could
not have done it
without the backing
of the CAP Charitable
Foundation, my
new family. On behalf
of the class of 2001,
thank you from the
bottom of our hearts.
Look for us in the
stars!"

William S. Chichester III
2001 Ron Brown Scholar

Julian Miller *(p.14)*
Winstonville, Mississippi
College Harvard University
Major Political Science

Macarrin Morton
Los Angeles, California
College Stanford University
Major English and Public Policy

Chrystal Obi
Sugar Land, Texas
College Rice University
Major Statistics and Biochemistry

Aliya J. Sanders
Bronx, New York
College Princeton University
Major Ecology and Evolutionary Biology

Eric S. Teasley *(p.108)*
Inglewood, California
College Stanford University
Major Chemical Engineering

David Adetokunbo Williams
Southfield, Michigan
College Harvard University
Major Cultural and Ethnic Identity Formation

Alexandra Carmel Wood *(p.62)*
Old Bridge, New Jersey
College Harvard University
Major Government

2004

Samuel Zenebe Alemayehu *(p.70)*
Beltsville, Maryland
College Stanford University
Major Biomedical Engineering and Math

Chaz M. Beasley
Conover, North Carolina
College Harvard University
Major Economics

Sharlene Brown
Bronx, New York
College Harvard University
Major Social Studies

Miya Nicole Cain *(p.38)*
Miami, Florida
College Yale University
Major (undecided)

Brent E. Cash *(p.34)*
Glenarden, Maryland
College Duke University
Major Mechanical Engineering and Economics

Preston Scott Copeland *(p.36)*
Baltimore, Maryland
College Harvard University
Major German and Economics

Tariq Dixon
Laurel, Maryland
College Harvard University
Major Social Studies

Caprice Gray *(p.10)*
New York, New York
College Yale University
Major (undecided)

Delbert A. Green II *(p.20)*
Opelousas, Louisiana
College Massachusetts Institute of Technology
Major Biological Engineering

Miles Alexander Johnson *(p.56)*
Oakland, California
College Harvard University
Major Social Studies

Sadé Lawrence
Lithonia, Georgia
College Georgetown University
Major Accounting and Finance

Jonathan B. Marable
Brooklyn, New York
College Dartmouth College
Major Biological Sciences/
Computer Science

Michael McDaniels
Hawthorne, California
College Stanford University
Major Mechanical Engineering

Crystal Paul *(p.60)*
Denver, Colorado
College Yale University
Major Cognitive Science and
International Affairs

Geraldine Pierre
Miami, Florida
College University of Virginia
Major Marketing and Finance

Samere Reid
West Palm Beach, Florida
College Harvard University
Major Social Anthropology

Kareemah Love Sabur *(p.28)*
Buffalo, New York
College Harvard University
Major History and Finance

Keaira T. Still
Lawnside, New Jersey
College Dartmouth College
Major Engineering

Victoria V. Tate
Compton, California
College Yale University
Major Biology and Classical Civilization

Carl Woodward
Fredericksburg, Virginia
College Stanford University
Major (undecided)

2005

Danielle M. Allen
Monroe, North Carolina
College University of North Caroline,
Chapel Hill
Major (undecided)

Naomi B. Andebrhan
Lakewood, California
College Stanford University
Major Human Biology

Sando Kpanah Baysah
Providence, Rhode Island
Harvard University
Major Biology or Math

Joseph Browne
Tampa, Florida
College Brown University
Major Computer Engineering

Mena A. Cammett
Brooklyn, New York
College Yale University
Major International Studies and Arabic Language

Reaha Campbell
Asheville, North Carolina
College Northwestern University
Major Chemistry

Lowell D. Caulder
Fort Wayne, Indiana
College University of Pennsylvania
Major International Business

Lindsay Lally Cothrine *(p.26)*
Bolingbrook, Illinois
College Yale University
Major Ethics, Politics and Economics (EPE)

Michael Crawford
Kissimmee, Florida
College University of Miami
Major (undecided)

Natalie Renee Davis
Detroit, Michigan
College Columbia University
Major (undecided)

Jordan Gilchrist
Stockton, California
College Stanford University
Major Political Science

Kristian J. Henderson
Little Rock, Arkansas
College Yale University
Major Biomedical Engineering and Ethics,
Politics and Economics (EPE)

Mondaire Jones
Spring Valley, New York
College Stanford University
Major English and Comparative Studies
in Race & Ethnicity

Jay Lundy, Jr.
Fort Pierce. Florida
College Harvard University
Major Government

Jeremy M. McGee
Hampton, Georgia
College Massachusetts Institute of Technology
Major Aerospace Engineering

Jeanine Pollard
Baltimore, Maryland
College Brown University
Major Neuroscience

Kai Ross
Davis, California
College Princeton University
Major Economics

Nicholas Anthony Smith
Miami, Florida
College Harvard University
Major Neurobiology or Molecular Biology

Robert J. Smith III *(p.64)*
Plantation, Florida
College Brown University
Major Urban Studies

Lynwood J. Walker
Hahnville, Louisiana
College Massachusetts Institute of Technology
Major Physics

"I look at every class
of Ron Brown Scholars
as my very own sisters
and brothers. We all
continuously care for
each other, and we
are always willing to
lend a helping hand
to others. When
I look at each Scholar
individually, I am
impressed. Just imag-
ine what we can
accomplish as a group.
The CAP Charitable
Foundation has made
it possible for me to
become a part of
something absolutely
great: the Ron Brown
Scholar family."

Geraldine Pierre
2004 Ron Brown Scholar

Acknowledgments

Christopher A. Pilaro

Vice Chairman, CAP Charitable Foundation

I Have Risen is a roadmap to hope and a blueprint for a better world.

It was made possible in part through grants from the CAP Charitable Foundation, but would be nothing without the Scholars who provided both the stories to fill its pages and the inspiration to publish it. We are exceedingly grateful to the essay writers for opening their hearts, minds, and lives to us so that we can better understand ourselves, our motivations, and our dreams.

Michael Mallory not only provided the nuts and bolts of the Ron Brown Scholar Program – he *is* the nuts and bolts of the program. Anyone who knows him will attest to the fact that Michael is a great teacher, a great friend, and a great man.

The Honorable John C. Thomas crafted his piece from the heart and with the honesty known only to someone who has been a part of the Ron Brown Scholar Program since its inception.

Sybil Fix organized the work into a beautiful journey and added poetry with every pen stroke she made.

The photographers Andre Lambertson, Joseph Rodriquez, and Clarence J. Williams III worked tirelessly and with amazing grace and vision to capture the true soul of the essay writers and provide a glimpse into what that risen soul might look like.

Lorraine Ferguson created an elegant book design that celebrates the Scholars and allows their work to shine through unhindered.

To all the Ron Brown Scholars, past, present and future, thank you for your enthusiasm for life and your desire to change the world.

Ron Brown Scholar Program

Michael A. Mallory
President,
CAP Charitable Foundation
Executive Director,
Ron Brown Scholar Program

Vanessa M. Evans
Associate Director

Fran Hardey
Executive Assistant

Kelly M. Raymond
Administrative Assistant

Selection Committee
Christopher A. Pilaro, *Chair*
Robert B. Binswanger
Thomas H. Boggs, Jr.
L.D. Britt, MD
Alma A. Brown
Michael A. Brown
Tracey L. Brown
Dr. Robynne K. Chutkan
Dennis F. Hightower
Mona K. Sutphen
Hon. John C. Thomas
Michael B. S. Treisman
Dr. E. Belvin Williams

Past Members
Maleka Donaldson Gramling ('98 RBS)
William H. Izlar, Jr.
Craigh Leonard
Anthony M. Pilaro
Linda C. Pilaro
Theodore W. Small, Jr.
F. Anthony St. Louis ('97 RBS)
Isabel Stewart
J. Paulson Tuffet ('97 RBS)

Research Fellows *(past and present)*
Ihotu J. Ali ('03 RBS)
T. J. Berrings ('00 RBS)
John Alexander Burton ('97 RBS)
William S. Chichester III ('01 RBS)
Kelly Cross ('97 RBS)
Shirley Delaleu ('98 RBS)
Maleka Donaldson Gramling ('98 RBS)
Immanuel R. Foster ('02 RBS)
Travis A. Gayles ('97 RBS)
Kara P. Hamilton ('99 RBS)
Karla J. Hardy ('01 RBS)
Alvin Ellsworth Hough Jr. ('02 RBS)
Amanda K. Johnson ('02 RBS)
Jacquelin S. King ('02 RBS)
Donielle N. Newell ('00 RBS)
M. Michelle Robinson ('97 RBS)
Maria I. Velazquez ('00 RBS)
Ellen Tachiewaa Yiadom ('02 RBS)

Volunteers
Brian Balogh
Susan Blackman
Julie I. Carrucio
Camille S. Cooper
Erika Cooper
Nicholas Duke
Joan Fenton
Yvonne Johnston
Barbara Kessler
Rebecca Lamb
Phyllis Leffler
Carolyn Livingston
Linda Miller
Kathie Morris
Parke Muth
Keith D. Roots
Steve Rubin
Charlotte Scott
Alexander Sedgwick
Charlene Sedgwick
Elsie Thompson
Mari Ines Woodsome

Council on African American Affairs

Michael A. Mallory
President

P. Amina Alio, Ph.D.
Senior Vice President for Research

Denise L. Dugas
Vice President for Development

Tami Abigador
Office Manager

Photography Credits

Andre Lambertson

pp. 29, 33, 39, 43, 45, 47, 49, 55, 61, 67, 69, 71, 73, 81, 87, 89, 95, 97,

Featured in *Time, US News & World Report, Life, National Geographic,* and *The New York Times Magazine,* Andre Lambertson's award-winning photojournalism has also been exhibited at the Smithsonian Museum, the George Soros Foundation, and the International Center of Photography.

Joseph Rodriguez

pp. 17, 21, 27, 37, 41, 51, 57, 59, 65, 75, 83, 99, 101, 103, 105, 107

Recognized with awards from the Rockefeller Foundation, the National Endowment for the Arts, and the National Press Photographers Association, Joseph Rodriguez has exhibited at Lincoln Center, the Corcoran Gallery of Art, the Stockholm Stadsmuseum, the Netherlands' Noorderlicht Gallery, the Leica Gallery in New York City, and at University of California/Berkeley, and New York University. His work has appeared in *The New York Times Magazine, National Geographic,* and *Mother Jones,* as well as in *Stern* and *Der Spiel* in Germany, and in *Esquire* in Japan.

Clarence J. Williams III

front cover, back cover, pp. 19, 23, 25, 31, 35, 53, 63, 77, 79, 85, 91, 93, 109, 111, 113, 115

A Pulitzer Prize-winner, Clarence J. Williams III has won national photography awards from the Associated Press and the National Press Photographers Association. He is a staff photographer for the Los Angeles *Times.*

CAP Charitable Foundation
1160 Pepsi Place, Suite 206
Charlottesville, Virginia 22901

Library of Congress Control Number
2005936584

ISBN 0-9772895-0-8

Distributed by
Ron Brown Scholar Program
1160 Pepsi Place, Suite 206
Charlottesville, Virginia 22901
Tel 434-964-1588
Fax 434-964-1589
www.ronbrown.org

Edited by
Sybil Fix

Designed by
Lorraine Ferguson

Printed by
Oceanic Graphic Printing

Front cover
Carmelle T. Norice (detail)
New York, New York 2005

Back cover
Samuel Zenebe Alemayehu (detail)
Stanford, California 2005

Printed in China